Beginner's G
Microcomputing

Beginner's Guides are available on the following subjects:

Amateur Radio
Audio
BASIC Programming
Building Construction
Cameras
Central Heating
Colour Television
Computers
Digital Electronics
Domestic Plumbing
Electric Wiring
Electronics
Enamelling
Fabric Dyeing and Printing
Gemmology
Heating and Insulation
Home Energy Saving
Information Technology
Integrated Circuits
Making Wooden Furniture
Microcomputer Languages
Microcomputing
Microprocessors
Minerals
Photography
Pottery
Processing and Printing
Radio
Spinning
Super 8 Film Making
Tape Recording
Technical Illustration
Technical Writing
Television
Transistors
Video
Videocassette Recorders
Weaving
Woodturning
Woodworking

Beginner's Guide to
Microcomputing

E. A. Parr
BSc, CEng, MIEE

Newnes Technical Books

Newnes Technical Books
is an imprint of the Butterworth Group
which has principal offices in
London, Boston, Durban, Singapore, Sydney, Toronto, Wellington

First published 1984

© Butterworth & Co (Publishers) Ltd, 1984

All rights reserved. No part of this publication may be reproduced or transmitted in any form or by any means, including photocopying and recording, without the written permission of the copyright holder, application for which should be addressed to the Publishers. Such written application must also be obtained before any part of this publication is stored in a retrieval system of any nature.

This book is sold subject to the Standard Conditions of Sale of Net Books and may not be re-sold in the UK below the net price given by the Publishers in their current price list.

British Library Cataloguing in Publication Data

Parr, E. A.
  Beginner's guide to microcomputing.
  1. Microcomputers
  I. Title
  001.64'04   QA76.5

ISBN 0-408-01221-8

Library of Congress Cataloging in Publication Data

Parr, E. A. (E. Andrew)
  Beginner's guide to microcomputing.

  Includes index.
  1. Microcomputers.   2. Microcomputers–Programming.
3. Basic (Computer program language)   I. Title.
QA76.5.P319 1984   001.64   84-1050
ISBN 0-408-01221-8

Photoset by Butterworths Litho Preparation Department
Printed in England by Thetford Press Ltd, Thetford, Norfolk

Preface

The growth of computer technology has been remarkable. In a mere 30 years computers have progressed from massive multimillion pound machines used by governments and large firms to cheap consumer items that can be bought by children with their pocket money (albeit with a little parental assistance).

The same technology has also brought about an information explosion, the most visible aspect of which has been cash dispensers and similar items. From banking to washing machines our lives will become intertwined with computers in one form or another.

Children do not share adults' suspicions of computers, and soon become adept at programming (as I have found to my cost). Education has tentatively adopted computers, an excellent step as computer literacy will be essential in the future.

This book has been written for people who have just purchased, or are about to purchase, a home computer. It is non-technical, and assumes absolutely no knowledge of electronics or mathematics beyond 2 + 2 = 4. It aims to rectify the omissions that most machine handbooks have.

There are several companion books in the Beginner's Guide Series: *Beginner's Guide to BASIC Programming* is a BASIC manual; *Beginner's Guide to Microprocessors* covers the hardware; *Beginner's Guide to Computers* covers computer science in general; *Beginner's Guide to Digital Electronics* covers the building block circuits of digital computers;

Beginner's Guide to Information Technology relates computing to communications; and *Beginner's Guide to Microcomputer Languages* compares the six most popular languages available on microcomputers.

I would like to thank all the firms who helped with information and photographs; these are acknowledged in the relevant places of the book. Many individuals also helped; special thanks are due to the headmaster and staff of Sir Thomas Cheyne Middle School, Sheerness, for helping me with the aspects of computers in education.

Finally, as ever, my long-suffering wife, Alison, in the age of the word processor, laboured at her typewriter to turn my illegible handwriting into intelligible and correctly spelt text.

E.A.P.

Contents

1 Introduction to microcomputing *1*
2 The microcomputer and its peripherals *21*
3 BASIC programming *58*
4 Not-so-BASIC programming *102*
5 Disks, files and records *144*
6 Games, graphics and sound *161*
7 Computer applications *189*
   Index *207*

It is desirable to guard against the possibility of exaggerated ideas that might arise as to the powers of the Analytical Engine. In considering any new subject there is frequently a tendency, first to overrate what we find to be already interesting or remarkable; and secondly, by a sort of natural reaction, to undervalue the true state of the case when we do discover that our notions have surpassed those that were really tenable.

Lady Ada Augusta, Countess of Lovelace

1

Introduction to microcomputing

'What is the use of repeating all that stuff', the Mock Turtle interrupted, 'if you don't explain it as you go on? It's by far the most confusing thing I ever heard'.

Lewis Carroll

From mechanics to mainframe to micros

The concept of a programmable computer was first conceived in the early years of the nineteenth century by Charles Babbage, a remarkable mathematician, engineer and inventor. Babbage's Analytical Engine, steam-driven of course, was purely mechanical and would have been the size of an aircraft hangar. Not surprisingly it never progressed beyond the drawing board, although a few, beautifully engineered, prototype parts can still be seen at the Science Museum in London.

If Babbage's ideas were impractical, it was because of the limitations of the technology of his time. His basic theory was sound, and every computer built since operates in a similar manner to the Analytical Engine. Realization of his ideas had to wait for over a hundred years when the arrival of electronics and the pressure of war lead to the re-birth of the computer in the mid 1940s.

A typical computer of this era would be based on thermionic valves (18 000 of these temperamental components in the American ENIAC machine), consume some 25 kW of electrical power and occupy the space of a reasonable-size house. It would be capable of storing a few thousand numbers, and could perform around a thousand arithmetical operations a second. Its cost (probably provided by the government) was well into six figures. A government report of this time concluded that 'it was unlikely that there would be the need for more than four or five computers in the United Kingdom'.

Valves are bulky, unreliable and consume a lot of power. The arrival of the transistor reduced the size of computers to the equivalent of a few large cupboards. This reduced size, improved reliability and, above all, greatly reduced cost and

Figure 1.1. An early valve computer: the Manchester University Mk 1 (courtesy Science Museum)

made computers a practical proposition for commercial organizations such as banks and insurance companies. One of the notable pioneers of commercial computing of this period was the British catering company J. Lyons (of Corner House fame) who developed their own LEO computer. The LEO company, through various mergers, eventually became part of ICL.

Computing remained expensive, and only within the reach of large organizations. It was also surrounded by an air of

Figure 1.2. The evolution of the building blocks of computer technology: relay, valve, transistor, integrated circuit, microprocessor

mystery and mystique, nurtured, naturally, by those involved in the industry. In the mid 1960s, firms such as Digital in the United States introduced a new breed of computers aimed at the small user. These were known as minicomputers. A typical minicomputer, such as the Digital PDP8 shown in Figure 1.3, was about the size of a television and cost a few

Figure 1.3. A minicomputer: the DEC PDP8 E (courtesy Digital)

thousand pounds and could be plugged into a domestic mains socket-outlet. Minicomputers were the first machines that could be used by individuals.

The real breakthrough came in the early 1970s with the development of miniature electronic devices called Integrated Circuits, or ICs for short. Originally developed for military missiles, these use advanced photographic and etching techniques to produce entire circuits on a slice of silicon a few millimetres square. Early valve and transistor

Figure 1.4. The microprocessor, showing the small physical size of the actual silicon slice within the integrated circuit package (courtesy Zilog)

computers were literally hand-built, but computers using ICs could use mass-production techniques. This, coupled with the cheap costs of the ICs themselves, brought a truly dramatic fall in the cost of a computer. In particular, an IC called a microprocessor was developed which contained about one third of the component count of a computer in one small 40-pin IC. Following on from the term minicomputer, it was natural to call a computer containing a microprocessor a microcomputer.

The price of microcomputers has fallen remarkably. The first microcomputers, such as the original PET, appeared in the mid 1970s and cost around £500–600. Early in 1980 Sinclair released their ZX80, the first widely available computer for under £100. Similar in power to early valve computers, this machine introduced computing to many people. The ZX80 was replaced in 1981 by the ZX81 which gave improved features (e.g. block graphics) for no increase in price. In 1982 the Spectrum, arguably the most popular microcomputer, gave sound, colour and high-resolution graphics, still for around £100.

It is therefore now possible, for a small outlay, to be the owner of a computer with a power that surpasses any machine that would have been a university's pride and joy just 20 years ago.

It has been said that we are at the start of a second Industrial Revolution; the term 'computer revolution' is often used. It is probably more accurate to call it an Information Revolution, since it encompasses not only microcomputers but related information services such as Teletext, Prestel and facilities such as bank cash cards.

In the UK, secondary schools can obtain a grant from the DOI (Department of Industry) for 50 per cent of the cost of a microcomputer under the government's MEP (Microelectronics Education Programme) scheme. Virtually every secondary school now has at least one machine, and the scheme is to be extended into primary schools. Computers in education is a topic we shall return to in Chapter 7.

Microcomputing has, rather surprisingly, fired the British imagination. At the time of writing, a remarkable one home in ten has a computer (and this does not include dedicated computers in games, washing machines, etc.). By the middle of 1985 it is expected that this figure will have risen to one in five. These are the highest figures of any country in the world, including the United States. It is probable that the UK is well on the way to becoming the world's most computer-literate society. This can be no bad thing, as a knowledge of computers will be essential in the future.

The computer revealed

In our increasingly technological society, we use many sophisticated devices without appreciating how they work. We drive motor cars without understanding what a Carnot cycle is, we watch television without worrying about quadrature modulation, and we use video recorders without knowledge of helical-scan recording techniques.

Although a computer is really a very simple device, some elementary knowledge of electronics is necessary to appreciate in detail how it works. As with motor cars, television and video recorders, however, we can use computers effectively with only a rudimentary idea of its operation. Most professional programmers have only a hazy idea of the electronics of a computer. We shall therefore describe a microcomputer in terms of functional boxes. Readers requiring a more electronically detailed description are referred to the companion book *Beginner's Guide to Microprocessors* which covers microcomputers from an engineering viewpoint.

In many respects, the operation of a computer is similar to the procedures followed by a clerk working at a desk (up to the middle of this century there were people actually called 'computers' who performed calculations under the direction of engineers and scientists. Babbage's original proposals for his analytical engine arose out of work with such 'computers' on astronomical tables).

Let us suppose we have a series of repetitive calculations to perform, and a willing clerk to help us. A typical job could be working out a series of electricity bills.

The clerk can be represented by Figure 1.5. He receives information (called input data in the jargon) which in our example will be a list of people's addresses and their meter readings. He is also given a set of instructions which tell him how to work out a bill. By following these instructions he can produce a series of bills (called output data).

The clerk and the equipment he needs are shown in Figure 1.6. Each of these is analogous to various parts of a computer, so it is instructive to examine them in a little detail.

We will need to communicate with the clerk, so our first

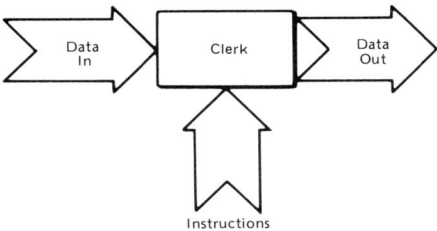

Figure 1.5. Symbolic representation of a clerk

item is an 'In Tray'. This will be used to supply the clerk with data to be processed (addresses/meter readings), and also to provide him with the instructions to be followed. We will also need to retrieve the output data (completed bills in our example), so we need an 'out tray'.

The clerk, sitting at his desk, will need to perform some arithmetic, so we will provide him with a calculator. He will also need some form of scribbling pad to jot down notes and

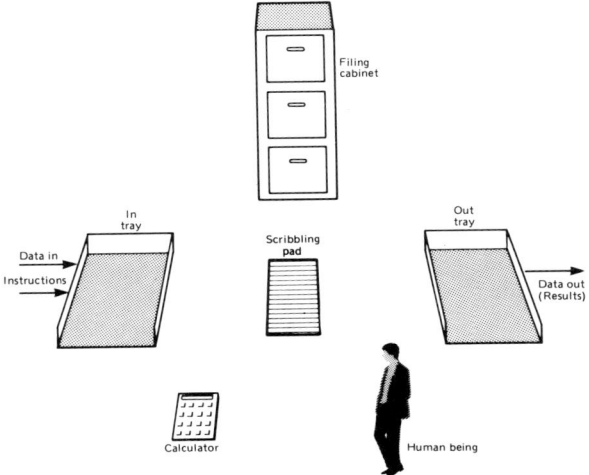

Figure 1.6. The equipment needed to do the job of a computer

partial results. Finally, he will need access to customers' records to obtain the last meter reading and details of any HP agreements or overdue accounts. These will probably be best kept in some organized manner in a filing cabinet.

It is likely that the clerk, in the course of his job, will be required to do many different tasks. Each of these will require a different set of instructions. It would be pointless to have to rewrite these each time a job is performed. The filing system is the logical place to keep a 'library' of standard instructions. To instruct the clerk to follow an operation for which standard instructions exist, we would simply say 'Get the instructions for job X from the filing cabinet and follow them'.

The items we need to provide our clerk with are therefore: (a) an in tray; (b) an out tray; (c) a calculator; (d) a scribbling pad 'memory'; (e) a filing system; (f) a set of instructions to follow. These will be 'controlled' by our clerk, who can now proceed to produce the bills for us.

Writing instructions

The instructions we provide for our clerk must be clear, concise and unambiguous. If the person we are writing the instructions for does not understand what is to be done, every step in the calculation must be clearly and rigorously defined. Let us assume the following rules apply to the electricity bill calculation.

1. Electricity units consumed is obtained by subtracting the last meter reading from the new meter reading. The last meter reading can be found on the customer's record in the filing cabinet.
2. Units cost 7p for the first hundred units, and 5p a unit for subsequent units.
3. There is a standing charge of £3.50 per bill.
4. HP payments are added to the bill. Details of HP payments can again be found in the customer's records in the filing cabinet.

Name D. Vader Address 57, Marsh Rd, Swale				
Date	Meter reading	Units used	Bill	Paid
23/10/83	27923	1852	113.10	✓
21/1/84	29719	1796	110.30	

HP Details
£15.00 / quarter until June 85

Figure 1.7. A customer's record card

5. Outstanding bills (from the customer's records) are to be added to the bill.

Customers' records are kept in the filing cabinet in a form similar to Figure 1.7. (This is known as a fixed-length record format, a topic we shall return to in Chapter 5.) To assist our clerk (who, it will be remembered, has no knowledge of what he is doing) we organize his scribbling pad into boxes as Figure 1.8. We can now write the instructions in the form of a 'flow chart' as Figure 1.9. By following this the clerk can work out the bill without needing to know what he is doing.

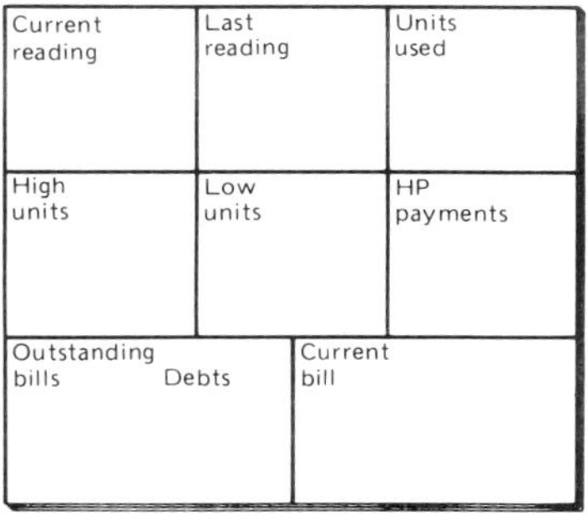

Current reading	Last reading	Units used
High units	Low units	HP payments
Outstanding bills Debts	Current bill	

Figure 1.8. Organization of scribbling pad

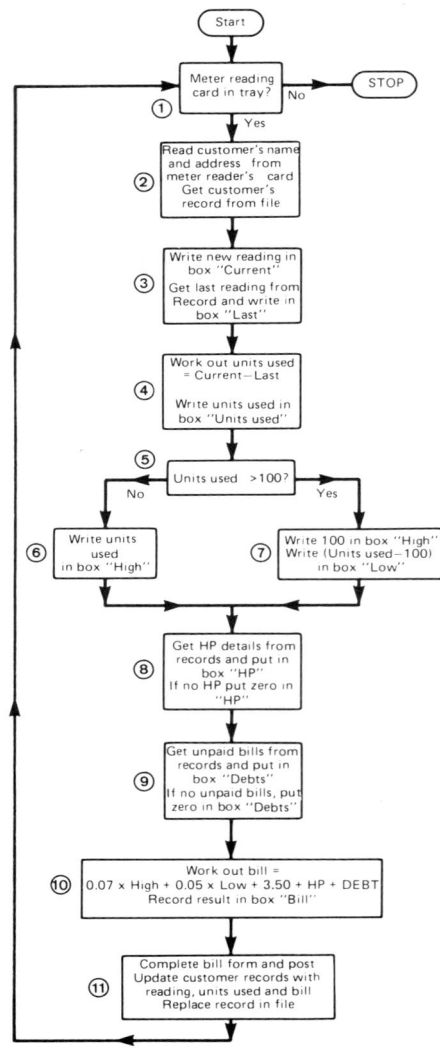

Figure 1.9. Flow chart for electricity bill calculation

This step-by-step approach is an insult to the intelligence of any human clerk, but is, as we shall see, directly analogous to the way we use a computer.

The electronic digital general-purpose programmable microcomputer

The microcomputer, in its full adjectival glory, is simply a machine performing the same task as our clerk.

● *Electronic* because it works with low-voltage electricity and devices such as transistors and integrated circuits.

● *Digital* because it works by operating internal electronic switches rather than varying voltages. In effect this means it deals with numbers in the form of a digital watch rather than in the form of a sweep-hand watch. A computer using variable voltages is called an analog computer; such machines are relatively rare nowadays. Digital circuits are easy and simple to build and very reliable. Compare, for example, the inside of an on/off light switch (which is digital) and a variable light dimmer (which is analog).

● *General-purpose* because its applications are limited only by the imagination of the user. The same machine can play games, work out the accounts for the local playgroup, keep VAT records for a small firm or act as a word processor. A computer which only performs one task (such as an in-car computer working out miles per gallon) is called a dedicated computer.

● *Programmable* is the most important concept to grasp. There are obvious similarities between a computer and a calculator; both use integrated-circuit technology; both are digital.

A calculator, however, only operates directly. If I wish to add 4057 and 3228 I will press the keys:

4 0 5 7 + 3 2 2 8 =

and the calculator will immediately give me the result 7285. You do not give calculators instructions as such (although some more expensive calculators can be made to follow a simple sequence).

In the electricity bill flow chart, we called for decisions at steps 1,5,8,9. A calculator, which only operates directly and immediately, cannot make decisions by itself. With a programmable computer a sequence of instructions is loaded into the machine, then the computer is told to follow the instructions. In following the instructions, the computer can make decisions and follow different routes through the flow chart according to the results it works out.

● A *microcomputer* is a computer based on a microprocessor, which is a small 40-pin integrated circuit similar to those in Figure 1.4. As we shall see shortly, a microprocessor replaces about one quarter of the electronic circuits of a computer. People who refer to the whole machine as a microprocessor are either misinformed or careless (so beware of computer shop assistants who try to sell you a 'microprocessor'. They should know better).

Contrary to popular belief, a microcomputer is not a super-powerful, revolutionary computer. All computers, even the elderly example of Figure 1.1 and the large mainframes used by banks, work in the same way (for people who like jargon it is called a Von Neuman machine).

In Figure 1.6 we identified the items necessary for a 'programmable clerk' to perform a task. They were, rearranged a little: (a) A method of inputing data and instructions. (b) A method of obtaining results. (c) A calculator. (d) Some form of 'memory' for holding scribbling pad results and some form of 'memory' for holding the instructions. (collectively called 'the store'). (e) A filing system for records. (f) A supervisor to read the instructions and manipulate items (a)–(e). This was the clerk himself.

Each of these items can be built using electronic components. How this is done need not concern us in this book. Readers requiring more information are referred to the companion books *Beginner's Guide to Microprocessors*, *Beginner's Guide to Computers*, *Beginner's Guide to Integrated Circuits* and *Beginner's Guide to Digital Electronics*.

A typical microcomputer is shown on Figure 1.10. This corresponds directly with the clerk and his equipment of Figure 1.6.

Instructions and information are entered via the keyboard. This can be considered as the in tray. Results can be viewed on the TV screen or printed out on the printer. These correspond to the out tray.

The filing system can be implemented either by floppy disc storage or the humble domestic cassette. These both provide storage for records or instructions when the computer is turned off. The store, arithmetic unit and control are all constructed out of ICs, and are usually contained on an electronics board called a printed circuit board (PCB) in the computer's case.

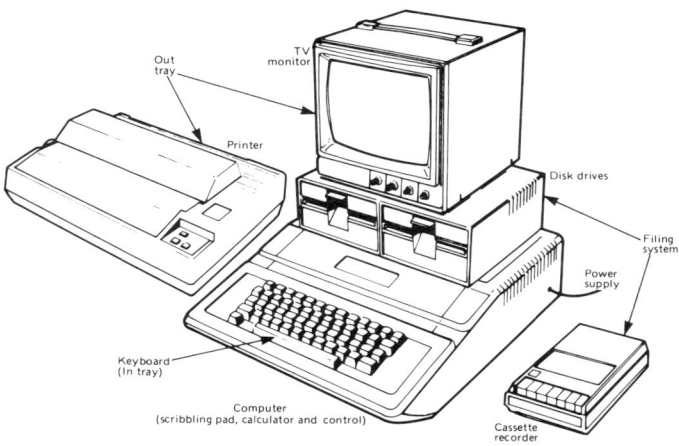

Figure 1.10. Parts of a microcomputer system

Historically, in older mainframe computers the store was housed in one cubicle, and the calculator and control in another cubicle called the Central Processor Unit (CPU). The microprocessor is simply the CPU of a small computer on one IC.

The final item in Figure 1.10 is a power supply. This is needed to convert the high-voltage alternating current mains electricity to the low voltage direct current electricity needed by the computer.

Using the store

Almost all the instructions we give to the computer will be concerned with manipulating data in the store. Data is a collective word for all types of 'information' we might be using: numbers (obviously), text (names and addresses for example) and displays for video games are all 'data'.

The actual construction of the store need not concern us, but we need some form of mental picture before we can use it. The simplest picture is a large block of pigeon holes similar

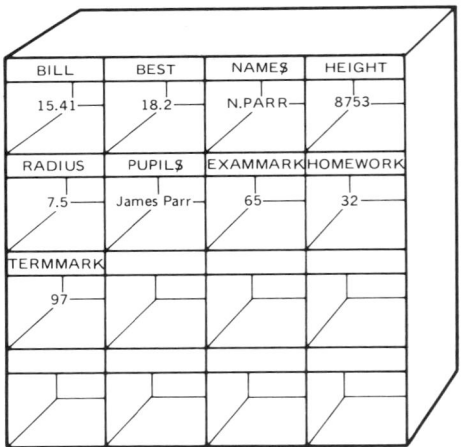

Figure 1.11. Representation of part of a computer store as labelled pigeon holes with typical contents

to Figure 1.11. We can put 'data' into the pigeon holes and retrieve it later. To do this we need to be able to identify pigeon holes.

The obvious way to do this is to number them with addresses 1, 2, 3 etc. This is actually the way the computer's electronics identifies them, but it is a little bit confusing for human beings, comprehending numerical addresses with numerical contents (e.g. put number 4057 in pigeon hole 3220).

Most computers allow us to attach 'names' to the store pigeon holes. The names can be anything we choose (with a few exceptions) so they can be made meaningful to us. The result of an electricity bill calculation can be stored in a pigeon hole called BILL. The highest score in an exam could be stored in a pigeon hole called BEST. A person's surname could be stored in a pigeon hole called NAME(a pigeon hole name with the dollar symbol as the last letter holds text in most microcomputers. The verbal jargon for HOUSE$ is HOUSE string, similarly Q$ is Q string, SCHOOL(is SCHOOL string).

Identifying pigeon holes with our own names allows us to write instructions such as:

- Put the number 8753 into pigeon hole HEIGHT
- Multiply the number in pigeon hole RADIUS by 3·1415926
- Check if the name in pigeon hole PUPIL$ is James Parr
- Add the numbers in pigeon holes EXAMMARK and HOMEWORK and put the result in pigeon hole TERM-MARK

In each case the names HEIGHT, RADIUS, PUPIL$ have been chosen by us, and the computer will choose its own pigeon hole numbers. HEIGHT may be pigeon hole 12736 but we do not need to know this; to us it is HEIGHT.

Using the value in a pigeon hole is often called 'taking' (e.g. take the value in CENT, multiply it by 9 and divide by 5). This is misleading as it implies that when a number or text is used it leaves the pigeon hole empty. In fact, using a pigeon hole leaves the contents unchanged. The contents are only altered when a new value is placed into the pigeon hole by an instruction.

It is a bit longwinded to have to refer to pigeon hole HEIGHT; in practice we just use HEIGHT. Our first example above simplifies to:

Put the number 8753 into HEIGHT

This can be made simpler still by using normal mathematical symbols:

HEIGHT = 8753

Similarly the last example above could be written:

TERMMARK = EXAMMARK + HOMEWORK

The store is also used to hold the instructions for the computer to follow. Figure 1.6 implies that the instruction store and data store are separate. Computers have been built with separate stores, but in practice it is restrictive. It would be quite possible, for example, to run out of space in the instruction store with the data store 90 per cent empty. In practice, therefore, the same store is used for both instructions data. We do not have to worry about this, as the computer control sorts out the store for us. (Usually some convention is adopted; one possible scheme is instructions start at the bottom and work up, data starts at the top and works down. Obviously the store is full when they meet.)

The process of writing the instructions to move data into the computer, manipulating it in the store and displaying the results is called 'programming', and the instructions themselves are called 'the program'. We shall return to programming in Chapter 3, and examine the various 'languages' in which instructions can be written in Chapter 4.

Stores are surrounded by a certain amount of jargon. The first of these is RAM, which stands for Random Access Memory. Each and every pigeon hole on Figure 1.11 can be accessed by the control with equal ease. It takes the same time to get a number from the first pigeon hole as it does to get a number from the last pigeon hole. Suppose we have a system where data is stored on a reel of tape. The time take to find a number on the tape will vary, depending on where the number is stored and where the tape is now. The latter system is called a Serially Accessed Memory. Because pigeon holes can be accessed randomly without delay, our microcomputer store is called a Random Access Memory.

Another common term is ROM, for Read Only Memory. As its name implies, this is a store in which the data in the pigeon holes is fixed and cannot be altered by the user. There are several places where ROMs are to be found, an obvious use being the holding of instructions for dedicated computers in washing machines, robots and similar devices. A common domestic application is the cartridges used in video games systems (which are themselves dedicated computers). All microcomputers, however, have at least one ROM. At power up a RAM store will hold rubbish, which raises the problem of how we get our instructions into the machine in the first place. All microcomputers use a ROM to hold instructions for a program called the 'operating system'. This program gives the computer instructions on how to read the keyboard and cassette, how to drive a TV display and similar essentials. Because the operating system is held in ROM it is not lost when the power is turned off.

The size of the store can be confusing: 32K, 4K and so on. This confusion is compounded by the fact that the store is used to hold the 'named' pigeon holes for data, the instructions (the program) and, in most machines, the 'picture' for the TV display.

The computer's electronics deals with very tiny pigeon holes, each called a store location. It takes several store locations to hold one number (typically 3–5 locations according to the machine design). It takes one store location to hold one letter (so it would take twelve locations to hold the text BRITISH-RAIL). It follows that the simple pigeon holes of Figure 1.11 are, in reality, blocks of store locations. This is yet another reason why we should refer to the pigeon holes by names and not bother ourselves with the actual store locations used.

The number of store locations on a machine is usually measured in 'K'. The strict definition of K is 1000, but in computing terms a K is 1024 (the reason for this odd value will be discussed below). A 32 K store therefore has $32 \times 1024 = 32\,768$ locations (note: locations, *not* pigeon holes).

Most microcomputers can handle a 64 K store, but the machine-operating system ROM must come off this (typically 8 K–12 K) and most machines use some of the store for the TV display (from 1 K to 20 K, depending on the detail displayed).

Usually the user will have between 16 K and 32 K of RAM for instructions and data storage. In general, the quoted memory size on computer catalogues is the RAM available for program, data and TV display (e.g. 4 K VIC-20, 16 K Spectrum, 32 K Dragon), i.e. the ROM space has been taken out before the figure for RAM is given.

Estimating the amount of store needed for a program and its data is not easy, but for beginners at least it is comforting to note that few simple programs need more than 8 K. For most users, with reasonable-size stores (upwards of 16 K), store space is not a problem.

1,10 buckle my shoe

Most people have heard that computers work in something complicated called binary. As was explained, it is not necessary to appreciate how a computer works to use it, so it is quite feasible to use a computer and write programs without having the slightest notion of what binary is. Occasionally, however, binary will surface in unexpected places (1024 being 1 K, 8 colours on a TV display are typical examples). In these cases a simple appreciation of what binary is, and why it is used, will usually explain an apparent oddity.

We are so used to counting in decimal that we rarely question it. Decimal is based on counting in tens, and is used by us because we have ten fingers! Had we evolved with eight fingers we would no doubt count in eights.

Each digit in a decimal number is a power of ten, so the number 8756 means:

	8 thousands	i.e. $8 \times 10 \times 10 \times 10$
plus	7 hundreds	i.e. $7 \times 10 \times 10$
plus	5 tens	i.e. 5×10
plus	6 ones	i.e. 6×1

If we had eight fingers, we would count eights using the digits 0–7. This is called an *octal* system. In octal the number 6134 means:

```
        6 × 8 × 8 × 8
plus    1 × 8 × 8
plus    3 × 8
plus    4
```

which is 3164 in decimal.

It is possible to construct a counting system based on any number. Most are only mathematical curiosities, but a system based on two, called *binary*, has some special advantages for computing.

The binary system has only two symbols: 0 and 1. A binary digit, i.e. a 0 or a 1, is called a *bit*. A typical binary number is 1101. This means:

```
        1 × 2 × 2 × 2    i.e. 8
plus    1 × 2 × 2        i.e. 4
plus    0 × 2            i.e. 0
plus    1                i.e. 1
```

1101 is therefore decimal 13.

A 4-digit binary number (i.e. a 4-bit number) can represent from 0 to 15. An 8-bit binary number can represent from 0 to 255. An 8-bit number is often called a *byte*. A 16-bit number can represent from 0 to 65535, and is usually called, rather confusingly, a *word*.

The most reliable and simple electronic circuits are those which only use two states (e.g. a high voltage or a low voltage). A common type of IC called TTL uses signals which can only be at 3 volts or 0 volts. It is very easy to design circuits in which one wire represents one binary digit; 3 volts, say, representing a binary 1 and 0 volts a 0. To represent any number between 0 and 255 we would need 8 wires. The resulting circuit is far easier to design than a circuit using, say, one wire and representing the number by a voltage from 0 to 25.5 volts in 0.1 volt steps. It will also be more reliable as electrical interference (a common trouble source) will have less effect on 3-volt signals than on 0.1-volt signals.

Internally, therefore, computers work in binary. The computer is arranged to accept and display numbers in decimal, which is fortunate since binary is both too cumbersome and confusing for everyday use. The binary operation does surface occasionally, however. A K (1024) is 10 bits; 8 colours is 3 bits; 64 K is 16 bits and so on.

Related to binary is *hex*, for hexadecimal. Hex is counting to base 16, which needs additional symbols to cover the decimal numbers ten to fifteen. Usually the letters A to F are used (so C is twelve, for example). A typical hex number is 3FE2 which means:

```
         3 × 16 × 16 × 16 = 12288
plus  F(15) × 16 × 16     =  3840
plus  E(14) × 16          =   224
plus     2                =     2
```

which is 16354 in decimal.

The attraction of hex is that conversion between hex and binary is a straightforward operation. The computer novice will have no need to use binary or hex directly, but should be aware of its existence. Encounters with features such as @% = 2020A (which is a hex number setting the print format in BBC BASIC) will then hold no terrors.

2

The microcomputer and its peripherals

A computing machine in action is more than the concatenation of relays and storage mechanisms which the designer has built into it.

Norbert Weiner

Choosing a microcomputer

At the time of writing, the cost of entering the world of microcomputing starts at the remarkable price of £50 for a ZX81 with a 16 K RAM pack to over £2000 for machines such as the IBM personal computer or the DEC Rainbow.

Trying to learn about computers without 'hands on' experience is rather like learning to swim without visiting a swimming pool. This is like Catch 22 for the beginner: to learn about computers you need to buy one, but being new to the game you do not have the knowledge to make a choice from the many machines on the market.

Choice is not made easier by the rather odd use of English in which the advertisers indulge. 'Superb styling' means grotty plastic case, 'professional keyboard' means squishy rubber keys, 'full range of peripherals' means we have a rough sketch of the circuit for a disk drive. Worst of all, 'allow 28 days for delivery' means lend us the money for at least six months to keep the banks off our backs whilst we get the bugs out of the prototype.

Although this may seem very cynical, history shows that Nascom, Oric, Sinclair and even the BBC have all been plagued by delivery problems. The first, and possibly the most important, rule in buying a computer is: if you can't buy it over the counter it does not exist.

The second rule in buying a computer is to be honest with oneself over motives for buying the machine. If it's for an insight into computing there is little point in buying anything other than the most basic machine for as cheap a price as possible.

A common reason for buying a computer is to provide children with a machine for their education. It is unlikely that the average child will be able to get more than a nominal access to a school's computer (even with the excellent MEP grant scheme) so the purchase of a home machine is an excellent investment for a child's future.

The choice of a machine in this case is very simple: buy the same machine as the local school. There are surprising differences in the way different computers operate, and it is most confusing for a child to use two machines with different dialects. For example, to position a character on the Xth position of the Yth line the BBC computer (very popular in schools) uses the instruction PRINT TAB (X,Y). Other machines use PRINT @ X,Y. Similar minor dialect differences exist all through BASIC, the language used in most schools. At the time of writing, schools seem to have standardized on four machines: the BBC Model B, the Spectrum, and the Research Machines 380Z and 480Z. The cost of the last two is a bit beyond the pocket of most people.

Probably some 70 per cent of home computer owners use their machines solely for games. For this application, good high-resolution graphics, colour and sound are needed. It is also advisable to have the facility to use joysticks. Using the computer's keyboard for the move/fire buttons in a 'Zap', the monster type of arcade game, will lead to the early demise of the keys. Joysticks are also more responsive to use. An important factor in choosing a machine for games playing is the availability, and cost, of games cassettes. Some excellent computers are blighted by an almost total lack of good games, and a positive feedback effect occurs where commercial software houses write games for the popular machines, and the popular machines are those which have games written for them! Graphics and games are topics we shall return to in Chapter 6.

Some adverts imply that a home computer can be used to run your burglar alarm, feed the cat or water the plants whilst you are on holiday, and run your central heating. Whilst feasible, such applications are not really practical or cost-effective. Connecting a computer to the outside world (called 'interfacing' in the jargon) requires a certain amount of electrical knowledge (and with mains-powered devices could be dangerous for the inexperienced). Connecting home-made equipment to a computer will almost certainly invalidate the warranty, and a ready-made interface board will cost more than, say, a complete purpose-built burglar-alarm control box.

People with an interest in the electronics/interfacing/hardware side of computing should consider a kit computer such as the author's first machine of Figure 2.1. Machines such as this come complete with full circuit diagrams and positively encourage add-ons. Construction of a kit needs some soldering competence, but is well within the ability of the average electronic enthusiast. Practical projects are music synthesizers, speech generators and model railway control.

Many programs are available for 'domestic management'. Home accounts, logs of freezer contents, medical diagnosis and menu and diet planning are typical examples. Unfortunately almost all of these are gimmicks and of little real use. It *is* possible to use a computer to keep track of and itemise the weekly shopping, but for most households a small notebook will work just as well. It should be remembered that for any accountancy or stock control program (which is basically what we are dealing with) to work, entries must be correct and consistent. The attention and time that such a home management program needs will rapidly become a chore (and that is without the interminable three- or four-minute delay whilst the program loads). If you are considering a computer to run your home, don't bother unless your home affairs are very complex. That is not to say that a microcomputer cannot have serious uses. Club membership records and accounts, yacht race results (with complex handicapping) and running a tote for a charity race night are applications that the author's machines have been used for.

Figure 2.1. A kit computer, the author's NASCOM, which is an ideal machine for people with an interest in constructing add-ons

Microcomputers can, however, be useful for small businesses, a topic we shall return to in Chapter 7. The same machine can be used for business during the day, and for education and family games in the evening. As an added bonus, the purchase of a small business machine is probably allowable against income tax.

Purchasing a business machine should be done as a complete package, i.e. computer, peripheral devices such as disk drives and printers, and the programs as one purchase from one supplier. In this way, the supplier will know what you intend to use the machine for, and be able to advise accordingly. You will also have some comeback if the resulting system does not meet your requirements. A recipe for disaster is to purchase a computer from one supplier, peripherals from another and a set of programs from a third.

Related to business machines is the use of the microcomputer as a word processor, again a topic we shall return to in Chapter 7. For now it will suffice to say that a word processor behaves as a super typewriter. Text is entered via the computer's keyboard and viewed on a television screen. Extensive editing facilities allow errors to be corrected and text added without the need for retype the whole page. Features such as automatic text centering are included.

There are several requirements to be met before a microcomputer can be used as a serious word processor. The first of these is a reasonable keyboard with typewriter-size keys. Small calculator-size keys (such as those found on the Spectrum or Oric) are not really suitable for the entry of large amounts of text.

The second requirement is a TV screen of at least 60 and preferably 80 characters per line. (A line of text on A4 paper contains about 70 characters with normal margins.) Displays with fewer characters per line will only be able to cope effectively with notepaper-size sheets. An 80-character display introduces another problem, however. Most domestic televisions do not have the capability to display small lettering; all that occurs is a slightly fuzzy multicoloured blob. A high-quality monitor is therefore required for serious word processing. It follows that the computer should be able to drive a monitor. For word processing, of course, a black-and-white monitor will suffice.

Text uses a lot of memory because each character (letter, numeral or punctuation) uses one store location. A single page of A4 paper will need between 2 and 4 K of memory. As the word processor program itself will need some 8 to 16 K of memory, a reasonably large store will be needed. Ideally, back-up storage, such as a disk drive, should be used.

Finally (and obviously) a word processor needs a printer. There are many different types of printer, and some are not suitable for word processing. This is discussed later in this chapter.

For most people, the choice of computer will be determined by the application for which it is to be used, the availability of programs, what machines friends have and above all cost. Technical considerations (such as which microprocessor is used) are of less importance than might be thought. The BBC Model B, for example, is a far better machine than the Sinclair Spectrum, but costs about three times as much. The question is 'is it worth the extra?' can only have a personal answer. If you want very high-resolution graphics or word processing the answer is probably Yes. If you just want to find out about computers, the answer is probably No.

Whatever machine is bought, it is inevitable that in a year something better will come along or the price will fall (to keep a particular model competitive with the opposition). Do not put off buying a computer for this reason; it has always been the fate of computers to be obsolete as soon as they are released. Waiting for a 'definitive' machine to come along is pointless, since there is always a better one just round the corner. Buy a computer when you are ready, buy the best you can obtain 'off the shelf' and have no regrets. Console yourself that you have a head start over people who wait for the 'Super Duper Mk 3' (who will probably have to suffer the bugs in the operating system that all new machines seem to have).

Getting started

Two vital accessories for a microcomputer are a tape recorder and a television (or monitor). A few computers have these already built in (e.g. the PET and Sharp machines) but this is reflected in the price.

Virtually any tape recorder can be used, although in general a mono recorder (which uses half the width of the tape) is preferable to a stereo recorder (which uses two tracks, each one quarter the width of the tape). It is not necessary to purchase a high-quality recorder; cheap portable units actually seem to give better results. So-called 'data recorders' or 'computer recorders' are often ordinary recorders in a different case at an inflated price.

There are a few desirable features to look for when choosing a tape recorder. The first (and absolutely essential) feature is output connections for an earphone or external speaker or line (for connections to another recorder or amplifier) plus input connections for an external microphone or line (for taking signals from another recorder).

A 'tape counter' is almost essential. It is prohibitively expensive to use one program per side of tape, and it is not possible to identify a program from its sound. With a tape counter, several programs can be stored on each side of a cassette and found again quickly and accurately. Incidentally, in the author's experience, it is not necessary to buy expensive, short (C10) so-called 'computer' tapes. Good-quality C60 tapes, which will hold about five or six programs per side, are more cost effective. C90 and C120 tapes are rather thin and should be avoided.

When loading programs into a computer, it is useful to be able to adjust both the volume and the tone (this applies particularly to bought programs, which vary considerably in quality). Volume and controls usually have no effect on the 'line' outputs (which are used for linking tape recorders, or for interconnecting a recorder and amplifier), so earphone or speaker outputs should be used if possible.

Most modern portable cassette recorders are equipped with an automatic record level, i.e. the recorder adjusts the signal recorded onto the tape. This usually works well, but it is sometimes useful to be able to set the record level manually. Ideally, but not essential, the recorder should have a selectable automatic/manual level setting and a record level indicator.

Standard recorder connections are shown on Figure 2.2. Earphone and microphone connections are usually via a 3.5 mm diameter jack plug. There are minor differences in length and in the depth of the tip recess which can occasionally cause problems. It is a good idea to take any cables provided with the recorder for comparison when buying interconnecting leads for the recorder/computer link.

External speaker connections are usually via the DIN connector (the word DIN does not, incidentally refer to the noise, it's the initials of the German Standards Institute). 'Line' connections are usually made via a 5-pin DIN connector or, less commonly, via phono plugs. There are two 5-pin DIN plug connections standards (one is the mirror image of the other) so it is advisable to take the recorder handbook when purchasing a DIN line/computer interconnecting lead.

Some computers provide a relay contact output which can be used to start and stop the recorder automatically. This

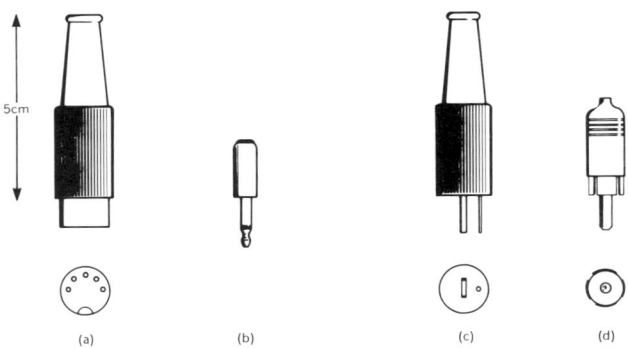

Figure 2.2. Common audio connectors found on tape recorders. (a) 5-pin DIN, used on line outputs. (b) 3.5 mm jack used for mic input and earphone output. (c) DIN speaker plug. (d) Phono plug

normally connects to the recorder via a 2.5 mm jack plug (similar in appearance to a 3.5 mm jack plug but slightly smaller) which is used in place of the remote stop/start switch fitted to some microphones.

Some computers will only work with their manufacturer's own recorders (Commodore and some Tandy machines for example). Although these recorders are specifically designed for their computer, and accordingly record and play back perfectly, they are usually more expensive than a domestic recorder. The purchaser should beware of such hidden costs.

Programs are stored on the tape as alternating high and low notes (sounding rather like a sharp-edged trill). 'Clicks' on the tape, caused, say, by an immersion heater switching, will cause errors. When recording, it is advisable to arrange that no high current loads elsewhere in the house are likely to switch on or off. Common villains are all forms of electrical heaters, kettles, dishwashers, fridges and washing machines.

There is nothing more infuriating than working for a few hours on a program which is then recorded with an error onto tape. A very desirable feature on a computer is a VERIFY (or similar) command which allows a recorded program to be read off the tape again and checked against the program in the computer. If the recording has not been successful, another attempt at recording can be made.

All microcomputers are designed to be used with a domestic television, and come equipped with a lead which plugs into the aerial socket on the television (rather confusingly, some computers use a phono plug connection at the computer end of the lead). Most computer outputs are tuned to be in the region of Channel 36 (which is also used by video recorders and TV games).

With the computer and TV connected and both turned on, it will probably be necessary to retune one of the buttons on the TV to get a clear picture from the computer. There are many different ways of doing this (each TV manufacturer has his own arrangements) but the TV instruction manual should give details of how the tuning controls work. When correctly tuned in, a simple message from the computer will be seen such as:

BBC Computer 32 K
BASIC
>

The arrow head > (called a prompt) means the computer is ready to accept instructions. Other prompts are used by other machines; common ones are square brackets], a flashing underline symbol _ or a 'blob' ■.

It is possible that the computer output will be found at several positions on the tuning control. The clearest position should be chosen. Often the computer picture is accompanied by a buzz from the television speaker. If this cannot be removed by the tuning control, it indicates a slight maladjustment inside the television which can be easily corrected by a service engineer. If the computer does not use the television sound itself (as does the Dragon), any spurious sound can be suppressed by turning the volume down.

The picture should be clear and stable, but colour fringing around edges is common and no cause for concern. If a clear picture cannot be obtained, it is best to take both television and computer back to the computer supplier who will be able to tell you which is at fault. The fact that a TV gives a reasonable broadcast picture does not mean it's the computer's fault if it fails to give a clear computer picture. If a second television is available in the house, this can be used to clear or implicate the computer.

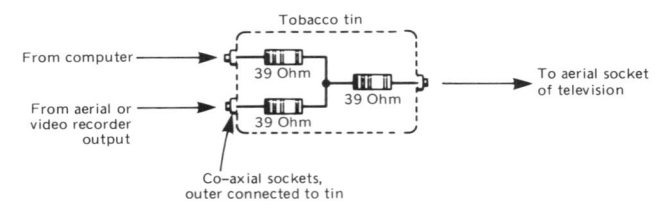

Figure 2.3. Simple home-made combiner circuit

It is not a good idea to keep swapping between the aerial lead and the computer. In a very short time, the socket on the television will loose its spring and give a troublesome bad connection. A signal combiner can be purchased for a small sum, which will allow the aerial lead (either direct or via a video recorder) and computer to be permanently connected to the television. Alternatively a combiner can easily be constructed as Figure 2.3. A bought or constructed combiner does reduce the strength of the signal from the aerial, which could be a problem in weak signal areas. A small amplifier can be purchased cheaply which fits in the aerial lead (before a video recorder, if one is used). Many video recorders use the same TV channel as the computer. If a combiner is used, obviously the video recorder and computer cannot be switched on at the same time.

The picture on a domestic television is adequate but not brilliant. It is not suitable, for example, for displaying the 80-character lines used for word processing. The picture limitations arise partly from the fact that most televisions are designed down to a price rather than up to a standard, and partly from the operation that the picture has to go through en route from the computer to the screen.

Transmitted television pictures go through a process called modulation to allow them to pass from the transmitter to the

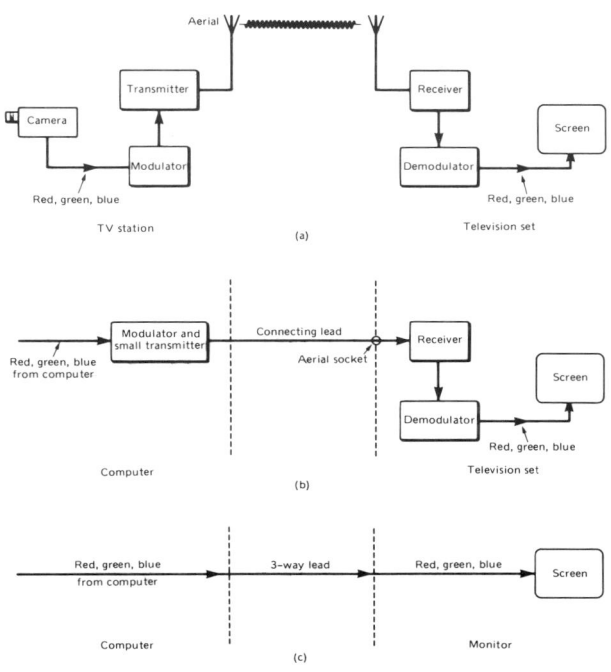

Figure 2.4. Driving televisions from a computer. (a) Broadcast transmission of TV picture. (b) Computer simulating broadcast signal. (c) Computer driving a monitor

house aerial. Inside the television the signal has to go through a demodulator to restore the picture. This process is summarized on Figure 2.4a.

Because the computer signal goes into the aerial socket, it has to look like a transmitted signal. Inside the computer, there is a small modulator, which converts the computer's signal to a form suitable for the TV. Inside the TV, the demodulator converts the signal back again. At each stage, a fair amount of quality is lost.

A television without a demodulator is called a monitor, and can take signals direct from the computer before the modulator as shown on Figure 2.4c. Note that three signals leads (red, green and blue) are needed. There is no loss of quality in transmission, so the resulting picture is far crisper than is obtainable with a domestic television. On the debit side, a monitor cannot receive broadcast services.

An obvious question is the feasibility of modifying a domestic television to bypass the tuner. This can be done, but is not a job for the amateur as there are safety considerations (not least of which is the fact that TV chassis are not earthed). It is interesting to note that some modern domestic televisions are being advertised with a monitor input for computer use.

Readers requiring more information on televisions and how they work are referred to the companion book *Beginner's Guide to Television*.

Using the computer as a calculator

With the computer and television connected and working, a few quick functional checks can be tried. The easiest are those using the computer as a calculator. It should be noted that the Sinclair machines use a single key entry for some instruction words. The word PRINT below, for example, is given by the single key press P on the Sinclair machines. On other machines it should be typed out letter by letter. Each line should be typed in, then the Return key pressed to tell the machine you have finished (on some machines the key is labelled Enter).

To use the computer as a calculator, the word PRINT is used, followed by the sum you wish to evaluate. The Return (or Enter) key completes the line, at which point the computer will give the answer. For example:

PRINT 3+4 (Return)

will give the answer 7

PRINT 5+12−6 (Return)

will give the answer 11

PRINT 5/6 (Return)

will give the answer 0.3125 because the / symbol means divide. The asterisk * means multiply, so:

PRINT 3.14*5/7 (Return)

will give the answer 2.24285714 (the number of decimal places may vary on different machines).

Brackets can be used to define the order of an ambiguous expression. For example, what would you expect for:

PRINT 3+5*2 (Return)

The computer gives the answer 13 because it is designed to do multiplication and division first, addition and subtraction second. Using brackets we can change this order. For example:

PRINT (3+5)*2 (Return)

will give the answer 16, and the more complex

PRINT (25+7)/((5+3)*5) (Return)

will give the result 0.8 because it is equivalent to:

$$\frac{25+7}{(5+3)*5}$$

It is good practice to use brackets if an expression is visually confusing, even if there is no ambiguity to the computer itself. The two expressions:

```
PRINT 17+(51*3) (Return)
PRINT 17+51*3 (Return)
```

both give the same answer, 170, but the former is clearer to the user. As we shall see later, clarity is an important part of writing computer instructions.

It will be obvious that the computer can be used as a very powerful (if not very portable) calculator. In the jargon we are using the computer in its Direct or Immediate Mode. We are not programming the machine, because the computer obeys our instructions as we enter them. Programming will be discussed at length in the following chapter.

Peripherals

'Peripherals' is the jargon for devices which are used for the input, output or storage of information. Technically, therefore, the keyboard, TV display and cassette recorder are peripherals. Usually, though, the term is applied to extras which can be purchased to enhance the computer.

The commonest peripherals are printers and disk drives. A printer can be used to obtain printed results (called 'hard copy') from the computer, but is really most useful for getting printouts of programs (called 'listings' in the jargon). The TV display on an average machine will show between 16 and 24 lines of a program at once. A large program will have several hundred lines, which makes it rather difficult to locate a fault by displaying the program on the screen. (It is also more comfortable to sit in an armchair looking through a program listing than sitting staring at a TV screen.)

Disk drives are the filing cabinets of the computer world. They provide vast amounts of storage space for information (such as membership records for clubs) and programs themselves. This storage is relatively fast; a large program can be loaded in a few seconds from a disk drive compared with several minutes from a cassette recorder.

Other common peripherals are analog interfaces, light pens and modems. In the rest of this chapter we will look at these, and other, peripheral devices.

Printers

For most people considering enhancing a microcomputer, the first choice usually lies between disk drives and a printer. In the author's opinion, a printer should be the first choice, because the use of disk drives implies the use of a lot of information and long programs which need a printer to view comfortably. Disk drives without a printer cannot be used to their full potential, but a printer on its own is useful for taking listings etc. (Ideally, of course, disk drives and printers should be purchased together, but that is a bit beyond most people's resources.)

Printers, like computers, have their own slightly confusing jargon, and with printers costing anything from under £50 to well over £1000 the choice can be difficult. A good rule of thumb is not to spend more on the printer than the original purchase price of the computer. In many cases there is little choice anyway, as some computers such as the ZX81 will only connect easily to the manufacturer's own printer.

There are many ways of classifying printers, but one that is often found is serial interface or parallel interface. There are 26 letters in the alphabet. To represent all the letters (in upper and lower case), numbers, punctuation marks, mathematical symbols and control functions (such as line feed, carriage return, bell etc.) requires over a hundred different characters to be recognized by the printer. In binary, this requires 8 bits, which are usually coded to the so-called ASCII standard shown in Table 2.1, which gives the decimal equivalent of the 8 binary bits. ASCII stands for American Standard Code for Information Interchange and is pronounced ask-key.

If we require 8 bits (which is effectively 8 signals) to send one character, we can achieve it in two ways. Figure 2.5a is probably the obvious way; 8 lines go from the computer to the printer, each line carrying one of the 8 bits of the ASCII code. Printers are, in computer terms, relatively slow devices so some form of interfacing is needed between the computer and the printer so that they do not trip over each other. In its simplest form, a signal from the printer will tell the computer

Table 2.1 ASCII characters

32		56	8	80	P	104	h
33	!	57	9	81	Q	105	i
34	"	58	:	82	R	106	j
35	#	59	;	83	S	107	k
36	$	60	<	84	T	108	l
37	%	61	=	85	U	109	m
38	&	62	>	86	V	110	n
39	'	63	?	87	W	111	o
40	(	64	@	88	X	112	p
41	)	65	A	89	Y	113	q
42	*	66	B	90	Z	114	r
43	+	67	C	91	↑	115	s
44	,	68	D	92	↓	116	t
45	-	69	E	93	←	117	u
46	.	70	F	94	→	118	v
47	/	71	G	95	_	119	w
48	0	72	H	96		120	x
49	1	73	I	97	a	121	y
50	2	74	J	98	b	122	z
51	3	75	K	99	c	123	{
52	4	76	L	100	d	124	|
53	5	77	M	101	e	125	}
54	6	78	N	102	f	126	~
55	7	79	O	103	g	127	

Codes less than 32 are control codes
7 Bell 8 Backspace
10 Line Feed 13 Carriage Return

that a character can be sent, and a signal from the computer will tell the printer that a character is waiting on the 8 signal lines. This interlocking is often called 'handshaking'.

Figure 2.5a is known as a 'parallel interface'. A less obvious method of sending the 8 bits of an ASCII character is shown on Figure 2.5b. Here, the bits are sent sequentially (one after the other) down one line. This is known as a 'serial interface', and is obviously simpler, but slower, than a parallel interface.

When connecting printers and computers it is obviously essential for them to match; not only on whether parallel or serial transmission is used, but also on voltages, connectors, the form of the handshaking, and the speed of transmission.

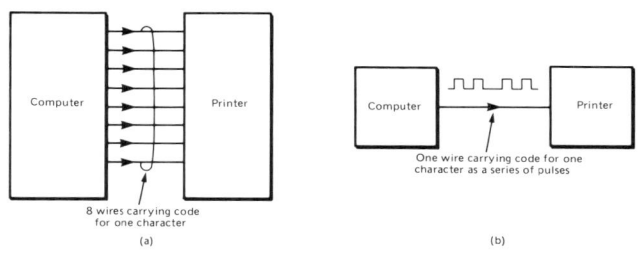

Figure 2.5. (a) Parallel and (b) serial data transmission

Parallel printers commonly use the so-called Centronics interface (called after one of the pioneer manufacturers of parallel printers). Serial printers use either the RS232 standard or the 20 mA current loop (the V24 standard and RS423 may also be encountered; for all practical purposes these are

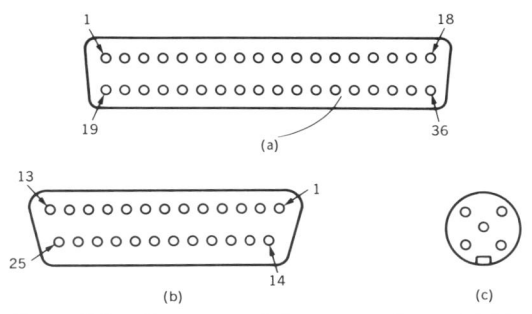

Figure 2.6. Common printer connections. (a) 36-way amphenol plug (Centronics parallel);)b) 25-way D connector (RS232 and 20 mA); (c) 5-pin DIN (for side view see Figure 2.2). Also known as domino connector (RS232)

identical to RS232). The handbook for a computer should state which standards are available on the machine.

Parallel printer connections are usually made via a connector called a 36-way amphenol plug (shown in Figure 2.6). It is usually easier to purchase ready-made connectors/leads, but standards are:

Pin	Purpose
1	Strobe (from computer)
2	Data 0
3	Data 1
4	Data 2
5	Data 3
6	Data 4
7	Data 5
8	Data 6
9	Data 7
10	Acknowledge (from printer)
19–36	Ground

Serial communications (both 20 mA and RS232) use a connector called a 25-way D-type plug (also shown in Figure 2.6). The standard connections for an RS232 signal appear quite complex:

Pin	Function	
1	Protective Ground	
2	Transmit Data	
3	Receive Data	
4	Request to Send	RTS
5	Clear to Send	CTS
6	Data Set Ready	DSR
7	Signal Ground	
8	Carrier Detect	DCD
20	Data Terminal Ready	DTR

Other pins are unused.

In practice, connecting a printer to a computer needs very few of these, the rest are used when connection is made to a modem (see later) or two-way communication is required (e.g. a printer with a keyboard). There are two possible options: with or without handshaking. These are summarized in Figure 2.7a,b. No pin numbers are given as computers and printers do differ between manufacturers (some, for example, reverse the functions of pins 2 and 3. Others use the domino connector of Figure 2.6).

There is no real standard for 20 mA serial communications, so the user should proceed with caution. Most printers use the same D-type connector as the RS232 standard, but with

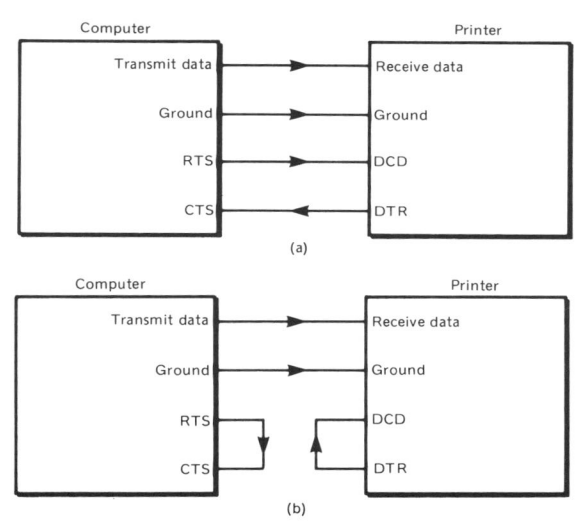

Figure 2.7. RS232 printers: (a) with handshaking, (b) without handshaking

different pinning and no handshaking. A common connection is:

Pin	Function
12	transmit −ve
13	receive +ve
24	transmit +ve
25	receive −ve

It will be gathered from the above that connecting a printer to a computer is not always a straightforward plug and socket job. If the reader is not prepared to use a soldering iron to make up his own leads, or is uncertain about the function of the pins on the connecting sockets on the printer or computer, the 'ad-hoc' purchase of a printer is not recommended. It is better to take the advice of a computer shop regarding the suitability of a printer for a specific computer, and invest in ready-made connecting leads. If there are any subsequent compatibility problems, the purchaser then has some legal comeback.

Problems can also occur if the computer sends characters at a different rate than the printer expects to receive them. The transmission rate is measured in *baud*; common standards being 110 baud, 300 baud, 1200 baud, 4800 baud and 9600 baud. For the technically minded, a baud is a transmission rate of 1 bit per second. The rough character rate can be obtained by dividing the baud rate by 10; 110 baud is about 10 characters per second (a fast typing speed). The commonest printer rate is 300 baud; about 30 characters per second. Few printers can *print* faster than 1200 baud, but some incorporate an internal store which allows them to accept characters at very high speed from the computer, the characters then being printed from the store at a slower speed. Obviously this can only work correctly if handshaking is used to prevent the printer store being overrun.

Another possible compatibility problem can a rise from an error-checking method called 'parity'. The details of this need not concern us, but in essence a check signal is added at the end of each character to ensure it has not been corrupted by noise en route. Parity can be unused, of positive sense or negative sense. It is important that the computer and printer agree as to whether parity is used, and if it is, which sense is to be adopted.

The reader is probably feeling a bit bemused, so by way of a summing up the electrical requirements for a printer to work are:

1. The same coding (ASCII is almost universal).
2. The same standard (Centronics parallel, RS232/V24, 20 mA serial).

3. Correct connections at computer and printer.
4. The same baud rate.
5. The same standards on parity (not used, positive or negative).

If there is any doubt, consult a local specialist shop.

There are many different ways in which a printer can operate mechanically, each with its own advantages and disadvantages.

Word processing requires good print quality similar to an ordinary typewriter. The best quality is obtained from the daisywheel printer, so-called because of the shape of the

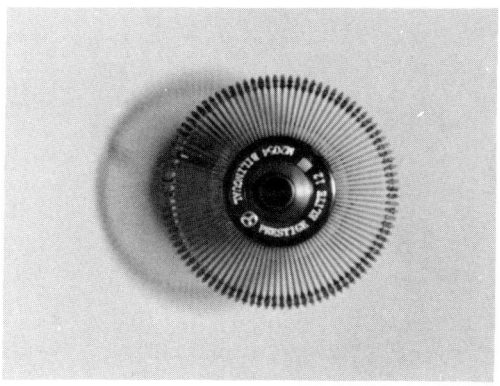

Figure 2.8. Daisywheel printer head

print head of Figure 2.8. The operating principles are shown in Figure 2.9. The characters are embossed at the end of the petals (with upper case, lower case, numbers, punctuation and other symbols, there are normally 96 petals). The wheel is spun at high speed until the required character is in position, then the solenoid-driven hammer strikes the back of the petal. The control is arranged to rotate the wheel as the carriage moves to the next character position, giving a relatively fast print speed (up to 300 baud being easily obtained).

The daisywheel printer has many advantages. It gives excellent quality, is reasonably fast and very quiet. Different sets or sizes of characters can be obtained simply by changing the wheel. Its major disadvantage is cost.

Where quality is not of paramount importance, a dot matrix printer will usually suffice. Any character can be

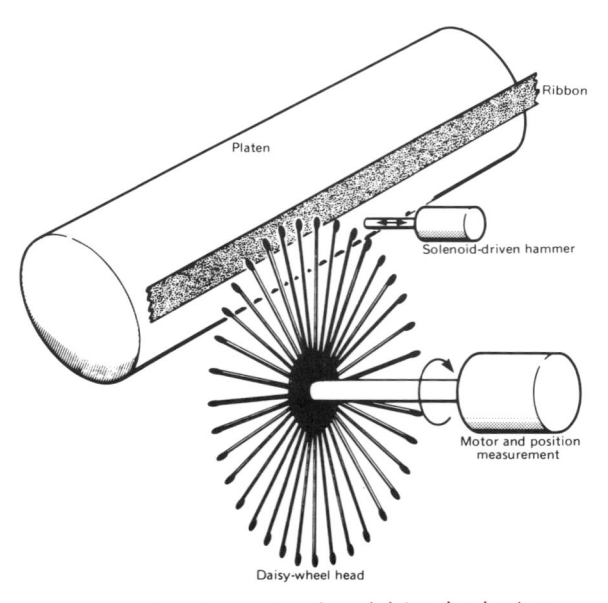

Figure 2.9. Operating principles of daisywheel printer

constructed from a pattern of dots called a matrix. Common arrangements, shown in Figure 2.10, use 5×7, 9×7 or 11×7 matrices. In general, the more dots in the matrix the less obvious the dot pattern will be. With a small number of dots, descenders (the tails on letters such as y and g) cannot be printed below the line, and the whole letter is lifted.

The operating principle of a 9×7 dot matrix printer is shown in Figure 2.11. The print head consists of a column of 9 needles which are driven by solenoids to hit the ribbon and

5 × 7   7 × 9   7 × 11

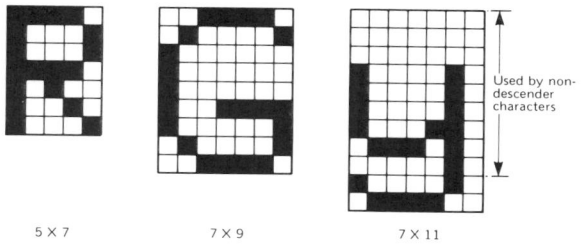

Figure 2.10. Various arrangements of dot matrices. 7 × 11 allows true descenders, most characters on 7 × 11 are confined to area 7 × 9

leave a dot on the paper. As the print head moves, the complete 9 × 7 matrix for each character is built up a column at a time.

The needles are fired by the solenoids at a very high rate (typically several hundred times per second). To reduce friction, fine capillary tubes are used with a ruby guide head. Figure 2.11 shows the solenoids arranged in a line for simplicity of illustration. In practice, the solenoids are arranged in a circle to keep the lengths of the needles similar and the head compact.

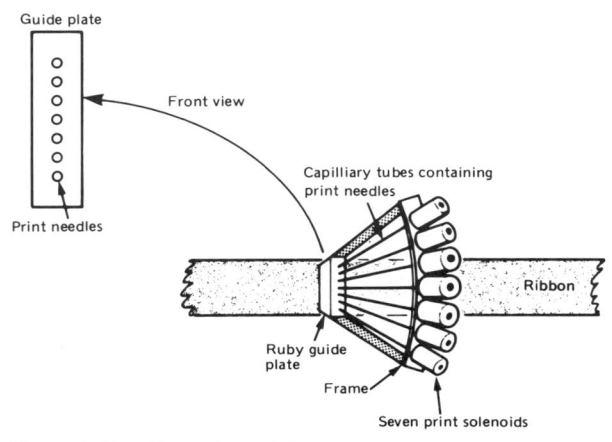

Figure 2.11. Operation of dot matrix printer

Matrix printers using a print ribbon can operate up to 1200 baud. Faster printing can be obtained by using a print head with no moving parts. Typical of these is the electrosensitive printer (of which the Sinclair printer is the best-known example). The print head has needles which do not move, but can be given a high voltage. The paper consists of an aluminium coating on black backing. If a needle is energized, a spark jumps to the paper evaporating a small amount of the aluminium to leave a black dot. Electrosensitive printers are small, cheap and very reliable (because they have no moving

Figure 2.12. Using a dot matrix printer in bit image mode

parts other than the head itself). The print quality is poor, however, and special paper is required.

Expensive dot matrix printers can also be used to reproduce graphics pictures from the computer. A typical example is shown in Figure 2.12. This facility is very useful in preparing business reports with graphs and pie charts for example.

A third type of printer, shown diagrammatically in Figure 2.13, is the drum graph plotter. The paper is attached to a

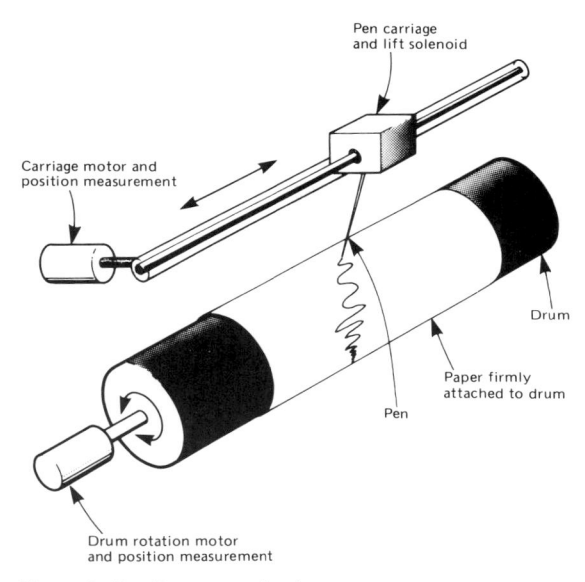

Figure 2.13. Drum graph plotter

drum which can be rotated in either direction to any position. The carriage carries a fine tip pen which can be moved to any horizontal position. By moving the drum and pen any character or symbol can literally be drawn. Between characters, the pen is automatically lifted off the paper. Although text can be written (albeit slowly), the graph plotter is mainly used for the preparation of graphs and charts.

There are other types of printers, known as comb, drum or chain line printers, which are used with mini and mainframe computers. These are very fast (up to 2000 lines per minute) but their size and cost preclude their use with home computers.

Disk drives

It does not take long to discover the shortcomings of using cassettes. The main disadvantages are time (it takes about 4 minutes to load a program) and the need for manual intervention because the computer has no control over the rewind/play/fast forward buttons on the tape recorder.

These shortcomings become even more serious when a cassette is used to hold information as a 'filing cabinet'. It is possible to hold 'files' on cassette (and we shall look at some techniques in Chapter 5), but the procedures to write and read data are cumbersome and slow. If, for example, we

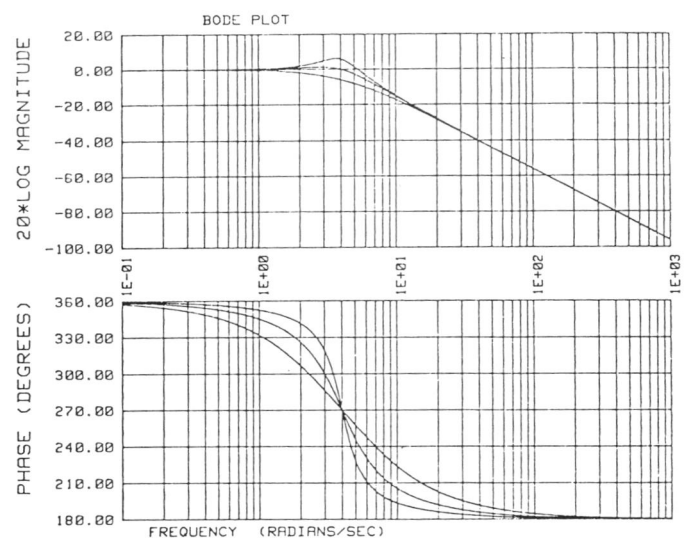

Figure 2.14. Example of drum plotter output

were using the computer to hold data on members and their yachts in a yacht club, we might want to know who owns the yacht with sail number 3220. To do this with cassette we would have to manually wind the cassette to the start of the file holding the details and let the computer work its way through the file, a process that could take several minutes.

An ideal filing system would be able to go straight to the required record with minimum delay and no manual intervention. Disk drives give this facility, and as an added bonus allow programs to be stored and loaded in seconds rather than minutes.

A disk drive stores programs and data magnetically on a specially coated circular plastic disk called a diskette. The diskette is permanently sealed into a protective jacket to prevent contamination or damage from scratching. The lining of the jacket is also specially treated to clean the surface of the diskette as it rotates. The diskette is flexible, and is consequently known as a floppy disk, to distinguish from the rigid metal disks used on mini and main frame computers. There are two common sizes of floppy disk, shown for

Figure 2.15.　20 cm and 13 cm floppy disks for microcomputers

comparison in Figure 2.15. The larger, 20 cm, disk is used on business machines. Smaller 3 in and 3½ in minidisks are also available.

A disk is organized into concentric tracks, which are further divided into sectors. The disk in Figure 2.16, for example, has 35 tracks, each of which has 10 sectors. Typically, one sector will hold 256 bytes of data or program (a total storage capacity of 80 K). Other common standards use 40 tracks and 80 tracks which give up to 400 K byte storage on a single disk. Double-sided disks (which can record on both sides) give up to 800 K byte storage. A movable read/write head is needed which can move to the required track. Some form of sector identification will also be needed so that data (or a program) can be loaded or written to the correct sector.

The components of a disk drive are shown in Figure 2.17. The read/write head is moved in the slot in the disk envelope to the required track by a device called a stepper motor. This

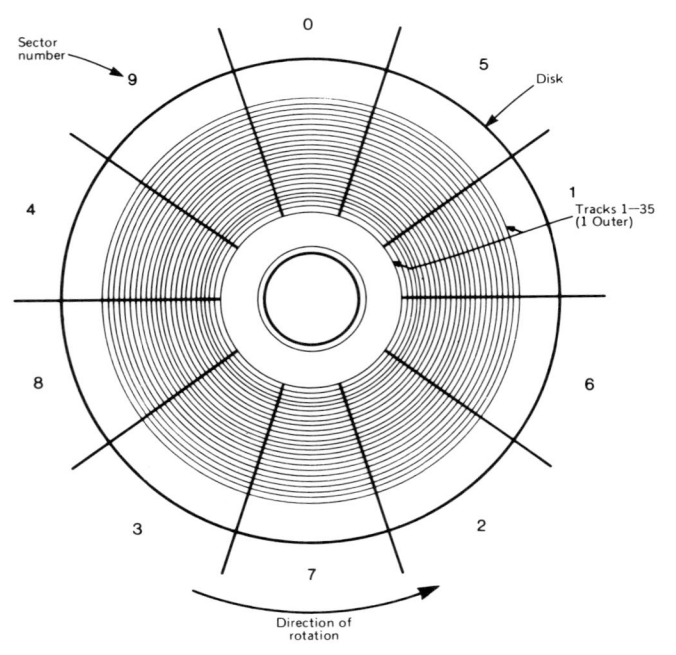

Figure 2.16. Tracks and sectors on a disk

ingenious device acts as both position actuator and position measurement. Sector identification is provided optically via a hole in the disk which is used to identify the starting sector. Sectors can be identified in two ways, called hard sector or soft sector. A hard sector disk has one hole per sector. Soft sector disks have one index hole to identify the position of the first sector, others being interpolated from the rotation of the disk. Most home computers use soft sectored disks with one hole.

To reduce wear, the disk is rotated only when data is to be read or written. The drive is taken via a hub spindle which is also used to provide sector identification by measurement of the disk rotation. Floppy disks rotate at 300 rpm. Protection against inadvertent writing is provided by the write-protect notch. If this is open, the disk can be written to. With the notch covered (by a piece of sticky tape), the disk is protected. The write-protect state is detected by a limit switch.

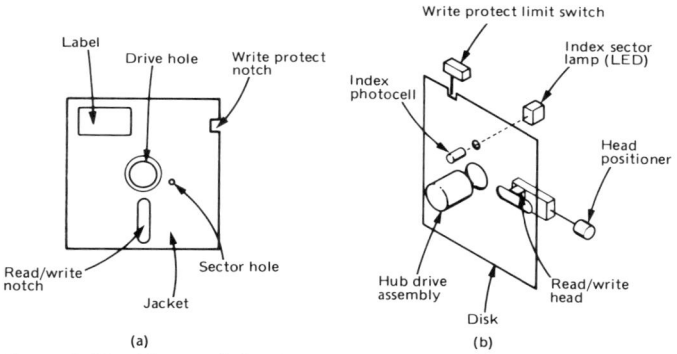

Figure 2.17. Floppy disk schematic: (a) floppy disk, (b) disk-drive components

All the items of Figure 2.17 are contained in a case similar to Figure 2.18, which shows a Tandy disk drive. This has a storage capacity of 83 060 bytes (rather limited storage by modern standards). The motor start time is 1 second, and it takes about 0.75 seconds to get the head to a track and wait for the right sector to come round. Data transfer can then take place at 12.5 K bytes/second.

The use of disks will be discussed at length in Chapter 5. A few practical points concerning disk use should, however, be followed at all times:

1. Keep the diskette in its wallet when not in use; Do NOT leave the disks in the drive.

Figure 2.18. Tandy disk drive. The spindle drive, head positioner motor and screw and index photocell are clearly visible

2. Do not smoke when using disks, since smoke causes a film to build up on the disk and head.
3. Keep disks away from magnets (e.g. motors, loudspeakers).
4. Write on the label with a felt-tip pen, *do not* use biros or pencils.
5. Do not touch the disk surface where it is visible in the read write slot.
6. Do not try to clean the disk surface, small scratches can ruin a disk.

Disks are not the only way of providing mass storage. An interesting variation is the so-called 'stringy floppy' which is actually quite an old idea popularized by Sinclair with their Microdrive for Spectrums and ZX81s.

Microdrives use a cartridge which contains an endless loop of tape, similar in principle to audio cartridges. These are essentially serial access devices; the tape has to be spooled to the correct place which can take about 5–10 seconds. A typical cartridge will hold 85 K byte and load a 48 K program in about 10 seconds. To the user, it can be used in the same way as a floppy disk.

Another alternative is the mini digital cassette shown on Figure 2.19 (which is part of an industrial control computer). The cassette and its associated deck are designed for storage of computer data/programs and provide full control of the tape start/stop/fast forward/rewind/record from the computer itself. The computer can locate, and load, programs with no manual intervention. Although slower than floppies and stringy floppies, the speed and convenience is far greater than a conventional domestic cassette. Mini digital cassette systems for home microcomputers are marketed under the trade name of 'The Hobbit'.

Light pens

A light pen is a cheap, but useful, peripheral to add to a computer. It is a small hand-held unit, similar in appearance to a ball-point pen. At its tip is a photocell which allows the computer to detect the point on the computer's screen at which the pen is pointing. From this simple idea, many useful applications can be developed.

A common use of light pen is literally as a 'pen' to draw on the screen and produce complex pictures which can be saved on a tape recorder or disk for future use. This requires a

Figure 2.19. Mini cassette and player with standard cassette for comparison

program to read, and follow, the pen position and draw on the screen, but most light pens come with a set of demonstration programs.

Another more businesslike application is in 'menu-driven' programs. Many programs contain choices or options for the user to select from a menu. For example:

Options are:

1. Enter competitor's details.
2. Print list of competitors.
3. Enter event result.
4. Print interim result.
5. Print final result.
6. Back-up current state to disk.
7. End session.

Enter option number –.

The user enters his option and the program continues, often to another menu. Option 3 above, for example, could request an event type if the program was being used to calculate results for a school's sports day.

Light pens are ideally suited for menu-driven programs. The pen is simply pointed at the option required, and the user does not need to be able to type. It is possible to enter data by having a numeric pad on the screen, for example:

```
7 8 9
4 5 6
1 2 3
0
```

and moving the pen to the numbers required in turn. This technique works best with the numbers displayed in inverse video (i.e. black on white) and well separated vertically and horizontally.

A related technique available on large mainframe computers, and some home computers, is the touch-sensitive screen. This detects the presence, and position, of a finger on the screen. A user simply has to point to the required option, number or whatever on the screen.

Light pens are surprisingly cheap, costing around £20 (which usually includes some demonstration programs). They are also an ideal DIY project for anyone interested in the electronics side of computing. To appreciate how a light pen works, it is necessary to appreciate how a computer TV picture is produced. This is discussed in some detail in Chapter 6.

Graphics tablets

A graphics tablet is used to transfer drawings from paper to the computer screen. In its simplest form it consists of a drawing board on which are mounted two movable arms which are fixed to the board on a swivel A and to each other by swivel B. The movable arms allow the head to be moved to any point on the board.

Swivels A and B have a simple device to measure the arm angles, which are sent to the computer via an analog interface (see below). The computer can then reproduce the head position on the screen by calculating the actual position from the angles via simple trigonometry. As the head is traced round a drawing, a simple computer program can reproduce

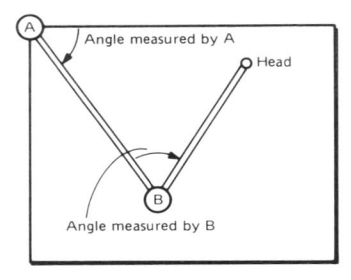

Figure 2.20. Graphics tablet

its path on the screen. An alternative, but more expensive, tablet senses a pen head position by a mesh of fine wires embedded in the tablet base. This allows a freely held pen to be used.

A related device is the 'mouse'. This is a small toy car-like device with position sensors mounted on its wheels. As it is rolled over a flat surface the position sensors signal its position to the computer.

Analog inputs/outputs

An analog signal is one that can have any value. Temperature measurements, speed measurements and position measurements are all analog signals. A computer deals only in on/off (or digital) signals. Before a computer can deal with analog signals, a device called an analog-to-digital converter, or ADC, is required to turn the analog signals into a digital form that the computer can use.

An ADC turns electrical signals into a digital number. We could, for example, measure a room's temperature in the range 0 to 100 degrees Fahrenheit with an electrical thermometer which gives a signal in the range 0 to 10 volts (68 degrees would be 6.8 volts). An ADC would convert the 0 to 10 volt signal to a digital number, say, in the range 0 to 10 000 (so 68 degrees would be 6800) which could then be handled by the computer.

The opposite process is required if the computer is required to, say, control the speed of a motor or the opening of a flow control valve. This is performed by a device called a digital-to-analog converter or DAC, which converts a digital number from a computer to an analog signal. Suppose, for example, we choose a DAC which takes a number from 0 to 10 000 and gives a signal in the range 0 to 10 volts and connect it to a motor which requires 10 volts for full speed. The number 1000 from the computer will cause the motor to run slowly, the number 5000 will give half speed, and 9500 nearly full speed. Any intermediate speed can, of course, be selected.

ADCs and DACs are often sold under the description of an 'analog interface board'. They are not the cheapest of peripherals, but are essential if the computer is to be used for, say, logging experimental results in a laboratory. Some computers already have some analog capability; the BBC Model B, for example, has four ADC inputs. A joystick input is a very simple, but not very accurate form of ADC. Most, but not all, microcomputers come equipped with joystick inputs. If accuracy is not too important, these can be used as analog inputs by people with some electronic knowledge.

Modems

The microcomputer is just one part of what has been called an Information Technology explosion. One major factor has been the ease with which computers and similar devices such as bank cash dispensers can communicate via the public telephone network.

The computer deals with on/off digital signals, and these cannot be transmitted directly over telephone lines. The on/off signals can, however, be easily converted to high/low tones which can be sent via the telephone. A device which performs the conversion from digital to tones (for transmission) and tones to digital (for reception) is called a modem (for modulator/demodulator).

There are basically two types of modem, although both fulfil the same purpose and connect to the computer via a serial interface, usually to RS232 standards. The cheapest modem is an acoustically coupled type which can be used with a domestic phone with no modifications. The unit has a cradle into which the phone handset can be placed. A microphone and speaker in the modem pass the tones to and from the handset. There is no direct electrical connection with the telephone network.

A direct connected modem is coupled electrically to the network and is usually arranged so the phone can be switched out (this does not stop the phone charging from clocking up, however!). Because there is no possibility of interference from extraneous noise, the direct coupled modem is more reliable than an acoustically coupled type.

The essential difference between these two types is shown in Figure 2.21. The telephone networks are understandably concerned about the reliability and safety of equipment connected to their lines, so direct connected modems have to be of an approved type. This approval increases the price. Acoustically coupled modems need no approval, and are more suited to the pocket of the home user.

With both types of modem, there are three ways in which data can be transmitted/received.

1. Simplex. Data can only be sent in one direction.
2. Half duplex. Data can be transmitted and received, but not at the same time.
3. Full duplex. Data can be transmitted and received simultaneously.

When used with a service such as Micronet (see Chapter 7), the modem is usually set for full duplex 75 baud transmit/ 1200 baud receive. A faster transmit speed is not required, because in most applications the data transmitted is being typed in from the keyboard and 75 baud will cope with the fastest typer.

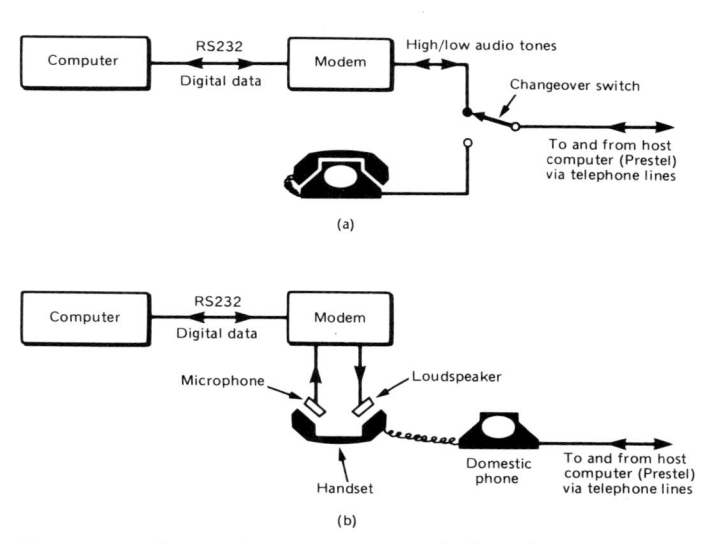

Figure 2.21. Connecting a computer to telephone lines. (a) Direct-coupled modem. (b) Acoustically coupled modem

Modems considerably expand the range of a microcomputer's abilities, giving access to services such as electronic mailboxes, electronic shopping, direct loading of programs from libraries and a whole range of facilities from Prestel to Micronet. The uses of modems are described further in Chapter 7.

3

BASIC programming

His faults are such that one loves him still the better for them.
Oliver Goldsmith
(with apologies to academic programmers who prefer structured languages)

Computer languages

To get any useful results from a computer we must be able to give it instructions. These instructions must be clear, concise and unambiguous. It is not possible, yet, to give a computer instructions in English ('Please give me a summary of last month's stock turnover'), and in any case English is rather an ambiguous language. The word 'or', for example, has two distinct meanings, as in 'Fix an appointment for Friday *or* Saturday' and 'You can add printers *or* plotters *or* disk drives to a computer'. The first use, incidentally, is called an Exclusive OR, the second an Inclusive OR.

Communication with a computer takes place in a language superficially similar to English with a smattering of mathematical symbols thrown in. There are many languages (some of which will be examined later), but the commonest in microcomputers is BASIC. This language was devised at Dartmouth College in the USA to introduce beginners to computing, and to act as a stepping stone to the 'professional' languages such as FORTRAN (as an aside, BASIC stands for Beginner's All-purpose Symbolic Instruction Code).

BASIC has surpassed its devisors' original intentions, and emerged from its educational background to become a commercial language in its own right. It has its shortcomings (some of which will be described later) and is somewhat passé with computer professionals, but it is remarkably easy to learn. It has become the standard language for home computers, although there are a few minor dialect differences between different machines.

This chapter does not aim to be a BASIC manual (for that the reader is referred to the companion book *Beginner's Guide to BASIC Programming*). There are many aspects of BASIC which are glossed over in the computer instruction manuals. This chapter aims to supplement these manuals by expanding on topics which often cause confusion. The next chapter introduces more advanced ideas such as structured programming, languages other than BASIC and machine code programming.

Introducing variables

Chapter 2 introduced the concept of a computer store as a set of pigeon holes with names that can be chosen by the user. These pigeon holes can be used to hold numbers (such as 57, −273, 2.5412, 1066) or text (such as 'Charles Babbage'). Text is known as 'strings' in the jargon, and we will examine how strings are used later.

Let us assume that we define some store locations as follows:

HEINZ	contains 57
COLD	contains −273
CMS	contains 2.5412
DATE	contains 1066
FIRST$	contains 'Charles Babbage'

The store, and its contents, can be considered as Figure 3.1 with our labels identifying the pigeon holes. Also in Chapter 2, we saw how the computer can be used as a calculator. Entering at the keyboard, for example,

PRINT 256*5 (Enter)

will give the result

1280

We can also manipulate store locations from the keyboard. As before, we are not *programming* the computer because it is obeying our commands as we type them in. To do this we use the BASIC word LET (on Sinclair machines this is obtained by the L key, on other machines it is typed in letter by letter).

To put the value 57 into a store location called HEINZ we type:

LET HEINZ = 57 (Enter)

This tells the computer to label the first available store location with the name HEINZ and put the value 57 into it (assuming no other location is already called HEINZ. If the location HEINZ already exists the value 57 would be put into the store location so named). Nothing exciting will be seen on the TV screen, however.

HEINZ	COLD	CMS	DATE	FIRST$	
57	-273	2.5412	1066	Charles Babbage	

Figure 3.1. Representation of variables in a computer store

We can now continue with the rest of the locations we named above. Each line should be finished with Enter (or Return). We shall leave 'Charles Babbage', however, until we discuss strings.

  LET COLD = −273
  LET CMS = 2.5412
  LET DATE = 1066

The computer's store (with the exception of FIRST$) now corresponds to Figure 3.1.

To see what is in a store location, the BASIC word PRINT is used. To see what is in location HEINZ we type:

  PRINT HEINZ

(remembering, of course, to finish the line with Enter or Return). This should give the result:

57

PRINT HEINZ tells the computer to print the value of the number in the store location called HEINZ. This does not affect the store location in any way, and does not alter its contents. If we type PRINT HEINZ again and again and again we will get 57 each time.

Similarly, we can get the values back from our other named locations

```
PRINT COLD
-273
PRINT CMS
2.5412
PRINT DATE
1066
```

If we ask the computer to PRINT the value of a name it does not know about, it will complain. For example, we have not used a store location called, say, BILL, so typing

PRINT BILL

will produce either an error message (e.g. No Such Variable) or the value zero depending on the machine used.

We can, of course, change the value of a location as often as we wish, as the following example shows:

```
LET TEST = 5
PRINT TEST
5
LET TEST = 74057
PRINT TEST
74057
LET TEST = 3220
PRINT TEST
3220
```

and so on.

It is a bit longwinded to keep referring to 'the store location with the name . . .' so the jargon word 'variable' is used. HEINZ, COLD, CMS, DATE, TEST are all called variables.

In Chapter 2 we used the computer as a calculator. We can use similar techniques to manipulate the contents of store locations (i.e. variables). For example, let us create two variables A, B (short names to save typing) and put the numbers 7, 15 into them respectively. To do this, we type:

```
LET A = 7
LET B = 15
```

Suppose we now type

```
LET C = A + B
```

This tells the computer 'Take the number in store location A, add the number in store location B and put the result into a store location called C'. Store location C (i.e. variable C in the jargon) contains 22 as we can discover by typing:

```
PRINT A
7
PRINT B
15
PRINT C
22
```

We can manipulate the values of variables with the usual four mathematical symbols + − * / and use brackets ( ) to define the order of calculation. For example:

```
LET A = 5
LET B = 8
LET C = 7
LET D = 3*(A+C)/B
PRINT D
4.5
```

Note that in the evaluation of D we have mixed a number 3 with the values of the variables. This is quite permissible.

Consider the rather odd-looking sequence below:

LET A = 6
LET A = A+2
PRINT A
8

The computer has given the result 8. Let us see how this is obtained. The first line is simple: 'take a store location, call it A and put the value 6 in it'.

The second line, in strict algebra, is nonsense. To the computer, however, it says 'take the number in the store location called A, add 2 to it and put the result back in store location A'. The result of this is, of course, 8 which is duly printed out by the third line.

So far we have been manipulating variables (i.e. store locations) directly from the keyboard; we have not been programming the computer. The concept of a variable is, however, at the foundation of all computer programming.

Before we can proceed to writing real programs, we should first look at the (few) rules which apply to the names we are allowed to use for variables.

Naming variables

The names given to variables should be chosen to be meaningful to the user. If we were, for example, writing a program to convert temperatures from Centigrade to Fahrenheit we could use a store location called CENT to hold the Centigrade temperature and FAHR to hold the Fahrenheit value, which would allow us to write the easily understood line:

LET FAHR = (CENT*5/9)+32

There are, however, a few restrictions on variable names. As usual there are slight variations between different manufacturers, but most follow the rules below.

1. The name must start with a letter (not a numeral or punctuation) but thereafter can contain any letter or number (but not spaces or punctuation)

Acceptable	Not acceptable	
AA	A A	contains space
B1	*B	starts with asterisk
TEMP2	2TEMP	starts with numeral

2. Names can be any length, within reason, but most machines only look at the first 2 or 3 characters of the name. The variables CARD and CART will be dealt with as one location, as the following sequence shows:

```
LET CARD = 875835
PRINT CART
875835
```

3. Names must not contain a BASIC keyword. A keyword is a word which tells the computer to do something; we have so far used two: PRINT, LET. The following possible names for variables would not be allowed:

LETTER, SPRINT, BILLET.

Other non-allowed names, using keywords we have not yet covered, are

| TOTAL | starts with the keyword TO |
| LIFT | contains the keyword IF |

Some computers do allow keywords inside a variable (and would accept LIFT). Because of these slight variations, it is best to check the instruction manual for a specific machine.

Printing messages

We have used the keyword PRINT to display the contents of a location (or, in the jargon, to display the value of a variable) as in:

```
LET YEAR = 1984
PRINT YEAR
1984
```

We can also use PRINT to display a message. This is of little use in direct (calculator) mode we have been using so far, but obviously needed in programs to display instructions and similar messages. Before we start to write programs in the next section, however, it is useful to see how messages are printed.

The message to be printed is simply enclosed in quotes " " and preceded by the keyword PRINT. For example:

PRINT "Hello Folks"
Hello Folks

The quotes tell the computer that what follows is a message and not a variable name. Note, for example, the effect of the sequence below:

LET TEST = 663333
PRINT "TEST"
TEST
PRINT TEST
663333

In the second line, TEST is treated as a message to be printed because it is in quotes. In the fourth line TEST is treated as a variable name, whose value is to be printed. It is very important to appreciate this distinction.

In the following section we will use the PRINT statement to construct some simple programs.

Programs and line numbers

Until now we have been using the computer rather like a calculator; we enter an instruction and it is obeyed immediately. In the jargon, we are using it in its 'direct' or 'immediate' mode. A *program* is a series of instructions which are entered into the computer, but not obeyed until we tell the computer to run the program.

The computer obviously will need to know which order the instructions are to be obeyed in, and (because no computer program works correctly first time) we will need some way to insert, modify and delete instructions. Both these requirements are achieved by the idea of 'line numbers'.

Each and every instruction in a BASIC program starts with a line number. This is simply a number which is used by the computer to identify the order in which instructions are performed, and by the user to identify instructions for editing purposes.

BASIC programs start at the lowest line number and work up in order. It is not necessary (or even desirable) for the line numbers to go 1, 2, 3 etc. Steps of 10 are usual, for reasons that will be obvious shortly. A typical sequence of line numbers would be 10, 20, 30 etc. BASIC simply takes the line numbers in ascending order, so the instruction with line number 10 would be obeyed first followed by that with line number 20 and so on.

This is all rather theoretical, and is best demonstrated with examples. First we must tell the computer that we are about to enter a new program. This is done by entering the command keyword:

NEW

We can now enter our program as below:

```
10 PRINT "THIS IS THE FIRST INSTRUCTION"
20 PRINT "THIS IS THE SECOND"
30 PRINT "AND THIS THE THIRD"
```

Note the line numbers; these tell the computer the order in which the instructions are to be obeyed. Note also that nothing has happened as we entered the instructions, the computer has stored them and is waiting for us to tell it to obey them.

Before we tell the computer to obey the instructions, it would be a good idea to check them. We can ask the computer to list our instructions by using the command keyword LIST (what else?)

```
LIST
10 PRINT "THIS IS THE FIRST INSTRUCTION"
20 PRINT "THIS IS THE SECOND"
30 PRINT "AND THIS THE THIRD"
```

To start the computer obeying the instructions, we use the command keyword RUN:

```
RUN
THIS IS THE FIRST INSTRUCTION
THIS IS THE SECOND
AND THIS IS THE THIRD
```

At any time when a program is not actually running, any instruction can be changed by simply retyping it. For example, let us change the message on the instruction at line 30. To do this we enter:

```
30 PRINT "THIS IS THE NEW LINE 30"
```

To see what we have done we LIST the program, and RUN it:

```
LIST
10 PRINT "THIS IS THE FIRST INSTRUCTION"
20 PRINT "THIS IS THE SECOND"
30 PRINT "THIS IS THE NEW LINE 30"
RUN
THIS IS THE FIRST INSTRUCTION
THIS IS THE SECOND
THIS IS THE NEW LINE 30
```

Instructions can be inserted between existing instructions by using suitable line numbers. An instruction with line number 25, for example, would go between lines 20 and 30.

```
25 PRINT "THIS IS AN ADDED LINE"
LIST
10 PRINT "THIS IS THE FIRST INSTRUCTION"
20 PRINT "THIS IS THE SECOND"
25 PRINT "THIS IS AN ADDED LINE"
30 PRINT "THIS IS THE NEW LINE 30"
RUN
THIS IS THE FIRST INSTRUCTION
THIS IS THE SECOND
THIS IS AN ADDED LINE
THIS IS THE NEW LINE 30
```

An instruction can only be inserted between existing instructions if there is a gap in the line numbers. It is for this reason that line numbers are initially spaced in tens. There is no disadvantage in leaving such spaces in line numbers.

Instructions are deleted by entering their line number on its own. To remove line 20, for example, we would enter:

```
20
LIST
10 PRINT "THIS IS THE FIRST INSTRUCTION"
25 PRINT "THIS IS AN ADDED LINE"
30 PRINT "THIS IS THE NEW LINE 30"
RUN
THIS IS THE FIRST INSTRUCTION
THIS IS AN ADDED LINE
THIS IS THE NEW LINE 30
```

Most computers incorporate additional facilities for making changes to instructions already entered into the computer. These allow typing mistakes, for example, to be corrected without the need to retype the whole line. Unfortunately these editing facilities vary tremendously from machine to machine, so it would be confusing to describe any specific editing method. The reader is strongly recommended to study how editing is performed on his machine; most, if not all, programs will have at least one error in them and good editing facilities save a lot of time.

Line numbers are an essential part of any BASIC program, so it is probably useful to summarise this section:

1. Line numbers are used to tell the computer the order in which instructions are to be obeyed. In the absence of any directions to the contrary (which we will deal with later) the computer starts at the lowest line number and works up in order.
2. Line numbers are usually (but not essentially) spaced in tens to give space for corrections.
3. Line numbers are used to allow insertion/deletion/correction of instructions (collectively known as 'editing').

Keywords

All instructions in BASIC start with a line number as explained above. The line number is followed immediately by a keyword which tells the computer what type of instruction follows.

We have already encountered two keywords: LET, which is used to change the contents of store locations, known, it will be remembered, as variables, and PRINT, which is used for printing the values of variables (as in PRINT SCORE) or for printing messages (as in PRINT 'EXAM RESULTS 1984').

BASIC has many keywords; most machines recognise those described below. In practice, the average user needs only a few; the rest can always be looked up from a machine manual when needed. This book is not intended to be an exhaustive study of BASIC (for that, the reader is referred to the companion book *Beginner's Guide to BASIC Programming*), so we shall only deal with the commoner keywords.

We have already dealt informally with the keywords LET and PRINT, so we shall start a study of keywords with a review of their function.

LET

The LET keyword is used to alter the value of a variable. This can be done directly as in

```
    LET DAY = 6
or  LET F1 = 2.9276
```

or as the result of mathematical operations as in

```
    LET AV = (A+B+C+D)/4
or  LET AR = 3.14*R*R
```

The right-hand side of the instruction can be of any desired complexity (and involve functions such as square roots, cosines and such which we will describe later). Mathematical symbols +−*/ may be used, and although not strictly necessary, brackets ( ) should be used to resolve visual ambiguities. In general, BASIC works out the expression to the right of the equals sign and puts the result in the variable to the left of the equals sign.

LET is the commonest keyword, and most BASICs (but not the Spectrum) actually allow it to be omitted. The statements:

```
LET R1 = A*A + B*B
R1  =  A*A + B*B
```

are identical in most BASICs. If no keyword is given most BASIC assumes LET was intended. LET is also used for handling text (strings), as we shall see later.

PRINT

The keyword PRINT has two main uses:

1. To display the value of a variable, as in

PRINT AV

2. To display a message, as in

   PRINT "PLEASE ENTER NAME"

After a PRINT instruction BASIC automatically starts a new line, so the simple program:

```
10 LET A = 47
20 LET B = 59
30 PRINT A
40 PRINT B
```

will give the display

   47
   59

The new line can be inhibited by the use of a semicolon ; at the end of the PRINT instruction, allowing us to write programs such as

```
10 LET A = 98.4
20 PRINT "THE VALUE OF A IS  ";
30 PRINT A
```

which gives the display

   THE VALUE OF A IS 98.4

A PRINT instruction can be made quite complex, and can involve variables, messages and even calculations all in one instruction as the following example shows:

```
10 LET F = 68
20 PRINT F;" DEGREES FAHRENHEIT IS  "; (F-32)*5/
   9; "DEGREES CENTIGRADE"
```

This gives a display:

68 DEGREES FAHRENHEIT IS 20 DEGREES CENTIGRADE

Note that there is no semicolon at the end of the instruction.

There are many other useful features available with the PRINT keyword. Tabulation (i.e. displaying numbers in columns), printing a defined number of spaces, printing to a user-defined format (e.g. XX.XX so 23.4712 is displayed as 23.47), printing at a certain column and row position (a feature we shall return to in Chapter 6) and, of course, printing to a printer rather than to a TV screen. Unfortunately these features suffer greatly from differences in dialect between machines, so description here could cause confusion. For example, the instruction to print at the 16th position on the 8th row is:

TAB(16,8)	BBC
PRINT@N	TANDY (where N = 455)
SCREEN 16,8	XTAL BASIC
PRINT AT 8,16	SPECTRUM

The reader is advised to study the small print on the use of the PRINT keyword on his machine.

In most BASICs, PRINT on its own generates a linefeed (i.e. it produces a blank (empty) line on the TV screen). This is useful for making easily readable displays.

PRINT with text variables (strings) is dealt with later.

INPUT

Most programs will require the user to enter data at some point in their execution. The keyword INPUT is followed by a variable, as in:

10 INPUT AGE

This instruction will prompt the user with a question mark ?. When the user types a number (and presses Return or Enter) the value is placed in the variable AGE.

Obviously the user needs to be told what he is expected to enter. One way to achieve this is to precede each INPUT instruction with a PRINT instruction. For example:

```
10 PRINT "WHAT YEAR IS THIS";
20 INPUT YEAR
30 PRINT "WHAT IS YOUR AGE";
40 INPUT AGE
50 Y1=YEAR−AGE−1
60 Y2=YEAR−AGE
70 PRINT "YOU WERE BORN IN  ";Y1;"OR ";Y2
```

When run, this would give the display:

```
WHAT YEAR IS THIS? 1984
WHAT IS YOUR AGE? 16
YOU WERE BORN IN 1967 OR 1968
```

In almost all BASICs, the PRINT instruction and the INPUT instruction can be combined in one line with the general form,

INPUT "message";Variable

so lines 10 and 20 above could be shortened to

10 INPUT "WHAT YEAR IS THIS";YEAR

Similarly, lines 30 and 40 can be shortened to

30 INPUT "WHAT IS YOUR AGE";AGE

There are some slight variations on the mixed INPUT/message instruction. On some BASICs (e.g. Tandy) the semicolon is mandatory. On others (e.g. BBC) the semicolon is omitted or replaced by a comma, in which case a question mark is added to the end of the message.

INPUT can also be used to obtain text from the keyboard, a topic we shall describe later. There are two related keywords, GET and INKEY, which are used to obtain a single character. These are mainly used for games playing, and are dealt with in Chapter 6.

GOTO
Earlier, it was said that BASIC uses line numbers to determine the order in which instructions are to be obeyed; unless otherwise directed the machine will start at the lowest line number and work up in order.

This can be changed by the use of the keyword GOTO (it should be noted that most BASICs do not allow a space between GO and TO, i.e. GOTO is one word and is obtained with one key on Spectrums and ZX81s). In its simplest form, GOTO is followed by a line number, as in

GOTO 20

which would cause the computer to obey the instruction at line number 20 (followed by the instruction after line 20).

A simple, never-ending, program using a GOTO to form a continuous loop, could be:

```
10 INPUT "GIVE ME A NUMBER";N
20 PRINT "FIVE TIMES   ";N;" IS ";5*N
30 GOTO 10
```

This will cycle on and on until the Escape or Break keys are pressed (which stop a running BASIC program and return control to the keyboard) or the machine is turned off.

GOTO is commonly used with the conditional keyword IF . . . THEN as we shall see shortly, which allows the program to follow different routes dependent on conditions chosen by the programmer. The GOTO keyword is one of the most useful in BASIC, but its use should be tempered with care. GOTOs, and particularly IF/THEN GOTOs, tend to proliferate and turn programs into a spaghetti-like nest of alternative routes. Spaghetti Programming will be discussed again later when programming style and Structured Programming are described.

REMarks
REM is a unique keyword, in that it (and all the lines it starts) are ignored by the computer. For example:

500 REM THIS LINE IS IGNORED

REM lines are used to explain the operation of the program and hence make it easier to understand:

1000 REM, THIS SUBROUTINE CALCULATES AVERAGE MARK

Although good documentation is essential, REM lines take up space in the computer store, and slow a program down a little.

IF . . . THEN

Any useful program will require some form of decisions to be made at strategic points. A club membership records program, for example, could be required to check if a member has paid his subscription.

Decision making is generally provided by the combined keyword IF . . . THEN, which takes the form

IF condition THEN instruction

as in the example:

IF A > 10 THEN GOTO 120

which means 'if the value of the variable A is greater than ten, the next instruction is at line 120, otherwise continue with the next instruction'. This is shown diagrammatically in Figure 3.2.

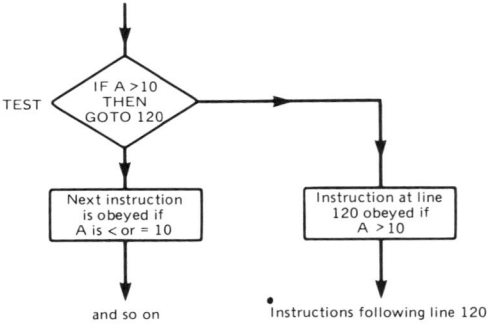

Figure 3.2. Diagrammatic representation of IF branch

The conditions are normally based on the values of variables and the tests:

```
=    equals
<    less than
>    greater than
```

These can be combined, as

```
<=   less than or equals
>=   greater than or equals
<>   not equal
```

Typical conditional tests could be

```
IF AREA < 10.5 THEN . . . . . . .
IF MARK <= 45 THEN . . . . . . .
IF TEST > LIMIT THEN . . . . . . .
```

Note that in the last example two variables are compared.

The instruction following THEN can be any valid BASIC instruction, but is often a GOTO instruction. Typical examples are

```
IF SUM > 10 THEN SUM = 0
IF EXAM <= 33 THEN GOTO 400
```

In the first example, if the value of the variable SUM is greater than ten, the value is set to zero (the keyword LET is assumed between THEN/SUM as explained earlier).

In the second example, if the value of the variable EXAM is less than or equal to 33, the next instruction is at line 400, otherwise continue with the next instruction.

The program below uses IF . . . THEN keywords to print out any multiplication table:

```
10 PRINT
20 INPUT "WHICH TIMES TABLE (ENTER 0 TO QUIT)";N
30 IF N=0 THEN GOTO 90
40 LET A=1
50 PRINT A;" TIMES ";N;" IS ";A*N
```

```
60 LET A=A+1
70 IF A <= 10 GOTO 50
80 GOTO 10
90 PRINT "BYE"
```

This program (which does *not* have particularly good style as it borders on spaghetti programming) has the structure of Figure 3.3. There is an inner loop (lines 50,60,70) which is executed ten times with A taking the values 1 to 10 inclusive.

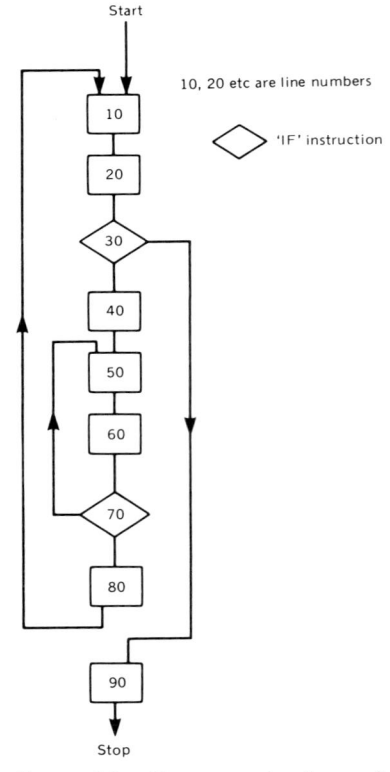

Figure 3.3. Diagrammatic flow of multiplication table program

Line number 30 gives the user the ability to stop the program by entering zero as a value at line number 20. More elegant ways of achieving this will be discussed later.

Line number 10 serves to separate each multiplication table from its predecessor and give a visually clean display as described under the description of the PRINT keyword.

Some machines support the more sophisticated structure

IF condition THEN instruction 1 ELSE instruction 2

If the condition is met, instruction 1 is obeyed. If the condition is not met, instruction 2 is obeyed.

FOR-NEXT

Repetitive loops similar to lines 50, 60, 70 in the multiplication table program above occur very often where a set of instructions are to be repeated a certain number of times, or data that is ordered (i.e. in tabular form such as employee time cards) is to be used.

Forming loops with IF/THEN is inelegant, and leads to programs that are hard to follow. BASIC allows loops to be constructed elegantly with the use of the FOR/NEXT loop.

In forming a loop we need:

1. A variable to count how many times we go round the loop; it is usual (but not mandatory) to use I or J or K. In the author's opinion, J or K are preferable because I can be confused with 1.
2. The starting value for the counter. This can be entered into the program as a number or obtained from a variable. Let us call this S.
3. The finish value for the counter. This can again be entered as a number or obtained from a variable. We will call this F.

The simplest form of loop is then:

    FOR J = S TO F
    Instructions in loop
    NEXT J

The instructions inside the loop are repetitively obeyed with the loop counter taking values from S to F inclusive (in steps of 1). The loop counter can be used (but not changed) inside the loop. The trivial program:

```
10 FOR K=2 TO 6
20 PRINT K
30 NEXT K
```

will give the display:

```
2
3
4
5
6
```

Using the FOR-NEXT loop we can write a simpler version of the multiplication table program:

```
10 PRINT
20 INPUT "WHICH TIMES TABLE (ENTER 0 TO QUIT)";N
30 IF N=0 THEN GOTO 80
40 FOR K=1 TO 10
50 PRINT K;" TIMES ";N;" IS ";K*N
60 NEXT K
70 GOTO 10
80 PRINT "BYE"
```

Apart from being marginally shorter, the above program is visually better and the loop formed by lines 40, 50, 60 is clearly defined by the starting FOR and the terminating NEXT.

As the loop counter variable can be used (but not changed) inside the loop, there are occasions where it may be useful to change it by values other than one each time round the loop. This feature is provided in BASIC by using FOR/NEXT/STEP which is used in the form:

FOR J = S TO F STEP P

where   J is the loop counter
        S is the starting value
        F is the finish value
        P is the amount by which J is changed each time round the loop.

S,F,P can be numbers, variables or expressions (e.g. MAX+2 where MAX is a variable).

The loop finish is defined by NEXT as above.

The trivial program:

```
10 FOR J = 3 TO 19 STEP 4
20 PRINT J
30 NEXT J
```

would give the display:

```
3
7
11
15
19
```

The step value does not have to be positive, as in

```
10 FOR J = 8 TO 2 STEP −2
20 PRINT J
30 NEXT J
```

which gives the display:

```
8
6
4
2
```

When the step feature is used, the difference between Start and Finish does not have to be an exact multiple of STEP. The loop will terminate when the loop counter variable equals, or exceeds, the finish. For example, the simple program:

```
10 FOR J = 2 TO 10 STEP 3
20 PRINT J
30 NEXT J
```

will give the display

```
2
5
8
```

(terminating because 8 + 3 = 11 which exceeds the finish value of 10).

The STEP value need not be an integer (i.e. it need not be a whole number). For example:

```
10 FOR J = 1 TO 5 STEP 1.32
20 PRINT J
30 NEXT J
```

will give the display:

```
1
2.32
3.64
4.96
```

terminating because 4.96 + 1.32 = 6.28 which exceeds the finish value of 5.

If STEP is not used, all BASICs assume a step of +1.

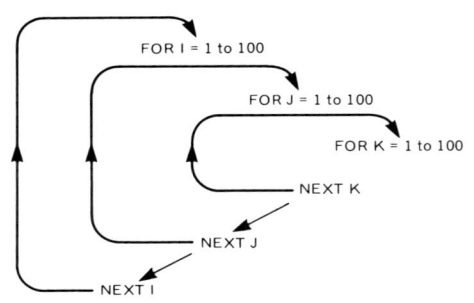

Figure 3.4. Cascaded loops. Inner (K) loop is obeyed 1 000 000 times

Loops can be cascaded within loops almost indefinitely as Figure 3.4. Care must be taken to avoid using the same variable for the different loops. A loop within a loop example is:

```
10 FOR J = 2 TO 5
20 FOR K = 1 TO 4
30 PRINT 10*J+K;
```

```
40 NEXT K
50 PRINT
60 NEXT J
```

The inner loop counter is K, the outer loop counter is J. This program gives the display:

21	22	23	24
31	32	33	34
41	42	43	44
51	52	53	54

The semicolons at the end of the PRINT instruction inhibits the standard new line after a PRINT. Line 50 forces a new line each time the outer, J, loop is obeyed.

A loop formed with FOR/NEXT keywords should only terminate when the loop counter reaches or exceeds its final value. Under no circumstances should a GOTO be used to exit from a loop. The following program is NOT allowed:

```
10 LET TEST = 4
20 FOR J = 1 TO 10
30 PRINT J
40 IF J = TEST THEN GOTO 60
50 NEXT J
60 PRINT 'DONE'
```

The above program will run as it stands, but as far as the machine is concerned the loop is still in progress. This will cause problems (often difficult to find) when an unfinished loop is part of a larger program.

GOSUB and subroutines

When writing programs, it is often found that similar blocks of instructions are needed at several points in a program. To save typing, memory in the computer and make programs easier to read, BASIC uses the idea of a subroutine. This is a set of instructions which are written once, but can be called from any part of the main program.

The operation of a subroutine is summarized in Figure 3.5. The keyword GOSUB is used followed by the line number of the subroutine, e.g. GOSUB2500 will call the subroutine starting at line number 2500 (so far GOSUB has behaved like a GOTO). The end of the subroutine is marked by the keyword RETURN which returns to the instruction following the GOSUB which invoked the subroutine. Calling a subroutine with a GOTO is not allowed. The RETURN instruction will cause an error message to be given if a subroutine is entered via a GOTO instruction.

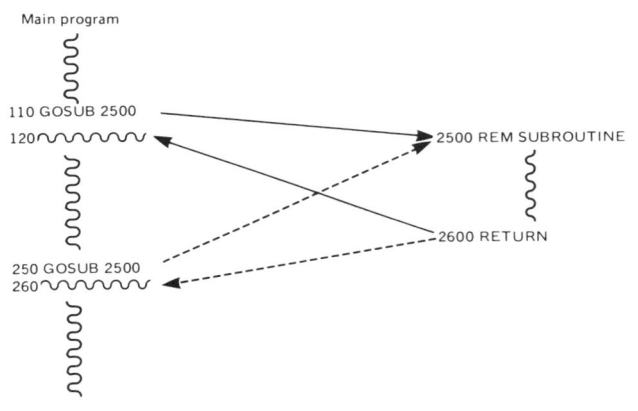

Figure 3.5. Operation of a subroutine

A subroutine can be called from many places. On Figure 3.5, for example, subroutine 2500 is called from line 110 (returning to line 120) and from line 250 (returning to line 260).

The rather contrived example program below gives the average of a set of numbers entered by the user. It uses a subroutine (at line 1000) to input the next number and check that it is in the range 0 to 99 (the numbers could be exam results, say).

```
10 INPUT "HOW MANY NUMBERS ARE YOU
ENTERING";N
20 IF N < 2 THEN GOTO 10
30 SUM = 0
40 FOR J=1 TO N
50 GOSUB 1000
60 SUM = SUM + A
70 NEXT J
80 AV = SUM/N
90 PRINT "AVERAGE VALUE IS ";AV
100 STOP
1000 PRINT "NUMBER ";N
1010 INPUT "VALUE ";A
1020 IF A > 99 THEN GOTO 1000
1030 IF A < 0 THEN GOTO 1000
1040 RETURN
```

In the above example, the subroutine is an idle luxury, but we have created a number input routine with error checking that could be called from elsewhere if our average program was itself part of a larger program. The number input subroutine can be used as many times as required by using the instruction GOSUB 1000.

We have introduced another keyword, the self-explanatory STOP at line 100. This stops the computer going into the subroutine when it has executed line 90.

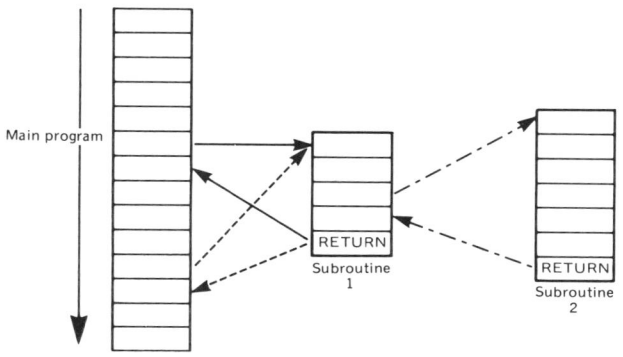

Figure 3.6. Nesting of subroutines

Subroutines can call subroutines and so on to any desired depth, as shown in Figure 3.6. This is called 'Nesting'. It is conventional and visually tidy, to put all subroutines at the end of the main program. Care must be taken to ensure that the main program does not accidentally run into the subroutines (as would happen in the example above if the STOP instruction was omitted).

Subroutines, and the related ideas of Functions and Procedures will be discussed again when structured programming and good programming style are described later.

Multi-instruction lines

BASIC allows more than one instruction to be put on one line provided they are separated by a colon : . The instructions are obeyed from left to right. For example:

```
10 LET A=3: LET B=5: LET A=A+B
20 PRINT A
```

will give the result 8.

It is not possible to GOTO the middle of a multi-instruction line. The whole line is obeyed.

Where a multi-instruction line contains a conditional IF, every instruction to the right of the IF is conditional on the result of the IF. For example:

```
200 IF N < 5 THEN M=M+1: N=0: A=0
```

the instructions M=M+1, N=0, A=0 are all conditional on the test N < 5.

Multi-instruction lines use less store and operate faster, but are visually less clear than assigning a line number to each instruction.

Real and integer variables

So far we have been dealing with what are impressively termed Real Numbers, which simply means numbers that can have a fractional (decimal) part. Machines differ slightly, but a typical BASIC will recognize positive or negative real numbers to 9 significant figures in the range 2×10^{38} to 2×10^{-38}.

Numbers with more than nine significant figures get truncated. For example:

| 3.14159265358 | becomes | 3.14159265 |
| 98758354657 | becomes | 98758354600 |

Note that although the number of significant figures is truncated the power of ten is correct.

Truncation can cause some odd results when numbers are tested for equality. Apparently innocuous programs such as:

```
10 A=3
20 B=6.4
30 C=9.4
40 IF A+B=C THEN PRINT "OK"
50 PRINT C
```

can misbehave because 3, 6.4 and 9.4 are all held with a slight truncation error. Even odder, the PRINT seems to give the correct result because PRINT corrects, to some extent, for truncations errors! (The above program might work correctly on some machines, but some other numbers will fail).

BASIC overcomes this problem, to some extent, by the use of integer variables. These are usually identified by a % symbol at the end of the variable name (e.g. BILL%). Integer variables can only represent whole numbers (i.e. no decimal parts) and the allowable range is limited (typically +2 000 000 000 to −2 000 000 000 although some machines only allow +32 000 to −32 000).

Arithmetic with integer variables is exact (providing they stay within the allowable range). Integer variables should obviously be used for all calculations involving money; the restricted range is no problem usually because it represents a resolution of one penny in £20 000 000.

Apart from accuracy, there are other advantages in using integer variables; they take less space in the computer's store and integer arithmetic is, in general, faster than arithmetic using real numbers. It is good practice, for example, to use integer variables as the loop counter in FOR/NEXT loops because the loop will operate noticeably faster.

Some BASICs allow a so-called 'double precision' variable which is, in essence, a real variable with greater precision (often up to 16 significant figures). Double precision variables are slower than normal real variables and use more space in the store.

String variables

We have previously covered two types of variable: real variables (the commonest type) which represent numbers which may have decimal parts, e.g. MAX = 2.937, and integer variables (with names ending in a % symbol) which can only hold whole numbers, e.g. I% = 15.

Computers are often required to work with text, i.e. a mixture of letters, numbers, punctuation, spaces etc., known in the jargon as alphanumeric characters. Names, addresses, descriptions of items in a works store are all examples where text is needed.

BASIC works with text via a third type of variables called String Variables. The names of all string variables end with a $ symbol, as in NAME$ or ADDRESS$ or TOWN$. Usually a string variable such as N$ is verbalized as N dollar or N string.

Simple text is enclosed in quotes " " and can be assigned to a string variable with a LET instruction. For example, the instruction:

LET HI$ = "Hello Folks"

puts the text "Hello Folks" into a pigeon hole labelled HI$, as represented on Figure 3.7.

This can be demonstrated by using the PRINT keyword, which when used with a string variable displays the text in the pigeon hole identified by the string variable. For example, if the LET instruction above is followed by:

PRINT HI$

the text

Hello Folks

will be displayed.

String variables can be entered from the keyboard using INPUT as described earlier for real and integer variables. Text entered via an INPUT instruction does not need to be enclosed in quotes. For example:

```
10 INPUT "Give me a boy's name";B$
20 INPUT "And a girl's name";G$
30 INPUT "Now give me some form of container";C$
40 INPUT "Now give me a liquid";L$
50 INPUT "Finally I want a part of the body";P$
60 PRINT
70 PRINT B$ ;" AND ";G$; " WENT UP THE HILL"
80 PRINT "TO FETCH A ";C$;" OF ";L$
90 PRINT B$; " FELL DOWN AND BROKE HIS ";P$
100 PRINT "AND ";G$;" CAME TUMBLING AFTER"
```

The text entered at lines 10 to 50 is held in string variables B$, G$, C$, L$, P$ and printed out in the relevant parts of the nursery rhyme at lines 70 to 100.

HI$
Hello Folks

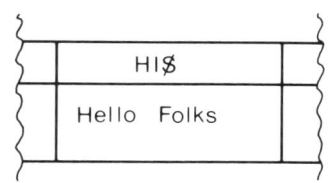

Figure 3.7. A string variable in the store

It is obviously not meaningful to perform mathematical operations on strings (what does CAT*DOG mean?), but strings can be combined using the plus sign, for example:

```
10 LET A$ = "CAT"
20 LET B$ = "FISH"
30 LET C$ = A$ + B$
40 PRINT C$
```

This will give the result

CATFISH

when run.

Manipulating string variables

Although it is impossible to perform arithmetic operations on string variables, BASIC does provide functions for comparing, splitting and using strings.

Comparison is based on the principle used in dictionaries, directories and indexes, i.e. comparison is done a letter at a time with A B C D etc. For example:

"ZULU" > "AFRICA" (because Z > A)
"AARDVARK" < "ABACUS" (because second letter in left-hand word is A, second letter in right-hand word is B)
"HOSKENS" > "HODSEN" (comparison taken to third letter)
"MELT SHOP MAINTENANCE" < "MELT SHOP PRODUCTION" (strings match as far as Maintenance/Production, when M < P)

With other symbols, punctuation < numbers < capitals < lower case. For the technically minded, ordering is, in fact, based on the values of ASCII code introduced in Chapter 2.

Tests for equality are easily made, as this possible extract from a games program shows:

```
1000 INPUT "DO YOU WANT ANOTHER GO";Q$
1010 IF Q$ = "YES" THEN GOTO 100
1020 IF Q$ = "NO" THEN STOP
1030 PRINT "UH?"
1040 GOTO 1000
```

The user enters a string as a reply to the question at line 1000. The string is held in Q$· If the string is "YES" we go for a new game (at line 100). If the string is "NO" we stop (at line 1020). If the string is neither YES or NO we respond (at line 1030) and ask again by going back to line 1000.

It should be obvious that a string is not a fixed length (most BASICs allow up to 255 characters in a single string). It is sometimes useful to be able to find out the length of a string by use of a function LEN. (LEN is called a function, not a keyword, because it operates on a variable directly and does not start an instruction line).

LEN gives directly the number of characters in a string variable whose name is given in brackets after LEN, e.g. LEN(Q$). For example:

```
10 INPUT "GIVE ME A WORD";W$
20 LET L = LEN(W$)
30 PRINT W$;" HAS ";L;" CHARACTERS"
40 GOTO 10
```

It is not possible (or meaningful) to directly mix real and integer variables with string variables. The instruction

```
LET AIM$ = SP + 5
```

for example, does not make sense (and would bring up an error message such as Type Mismatch if included in a program).

A string starting with numbers (e.g. '52, Railway Cuttings' or '23rd January') can have the numeric part converted to a number which can be used by a real or integer variable via the function VAL. Like LEN function, the relevant string variable name is enclosed in brackets (e.g. VAL(NAME$)).

The VAL function gives the numeric value of the *leading* characters. For example:

```
10 LET STREET$ = "52 RAILWAY CUTTINGS"
20 LET NUM = VAL(STREET$)
30 PRINT NUM
```

would give 52.

If the string has no *leading* numerals, VAL gives the value of zero. The program below can be used to examine the operation of VAL:

```
10 INPUT "GIVE ME A STRING";Q$
20 N = VAL(Q$)
30 PRINT N
40 GOTO 10
```

If Q$ is "6 WOOD", 6 would be displayed. If Q$ is "ETA 2100", 0 would be displayed (because the leading characters are letters). If Q$ is "1760 MPH", 1760 would be displayed.

It is important to realise that VAL operates only on *leading* numerals. It does not operate on embedded or trailing numerals; in these circumstances VAL returns zero.

A number can be converted to string form by use of the function STR$, although this is relatively infrequently required. For example:

```
10 INPUT "ROAD NUMBER";N
20 INPUT "STREET NAME";ST$
30 N$ = STR$(N)
40 AD$ = N$+" "+ ST$
50 PRINT "ADDRESS IS ";AD$
```

Strings can be dissected with the function LEFT$, RIGHT$ and MID$. LEFT$ allows a specified number of characters to be extracted from the left-hand end of a specified string. For example:

LEFT$(Q$,5)

where Q$ is the variable's name and 5 is the number of characters. The number of characters can be specified via a variable as shown in the demonstration program below:

```
10 INPUT "GIVE ME A STRING";Q$
20 INPUT "HOW MANY LETTERS";N
30 R$ = LEFT$(Q$,N)
40 PRINT R$
50 GOTO 10
```

If Q$ is "MIDSHIPMAN" and N is entered as 3, MID would be displayed.

A common use of LEFT$ is to simplify Yes/No inputs as the user can answer YES/NO as simply Y/N. LEFT$ is used to test the first letter of the users reply. For example:

```
1000 INPUT "ANOTHER GO";Q$
1010 IF LEFT$(Q$,1) = "Y" THEN GOTO 100
1020 IF LEFT$(Q$,1) = "N" THEN STOP
1030 PRINT "EH?"
```

RIGHT$ (rather obviously) allows a specified number of characters to be extracted from the right hand end of a string.

The format, and use, is the same as LEFT$. For example: if CLUB$ holds "3 WOOD" then RIGHT$(CLUB$,4) would give "WOOD".

Text can be extracted from the middle of a string with the function MID$. To use this, the string name is specified followed by the character position of the first character to be copied, followed by the number of characters. For example:

MID$(PUPIL$,5,4)

would give the four characters from PUPIL$ starting at character position 5.

Suppose TEST$ = "MAGISTRATES". Then MID$(TEST$,7,4) would be "RATE", MID$(TEST$,4,2) would be "IS", and so on.

As before, the starting position and number of characters can be specified by variables, as in the program below which will remove any given character from a given string:

```
 10 INPUT "GIVE ME A STRING";Q$
 20 INPUT "WHICH LETTER TO BE REMOVED";A$
 30 A$ = LEFT$(A$,1)
 40 L = LEN(Q$)
 50 B$ = " "
 60 FOR J = 1 TO L
 70 IF MID$(Q$,J,1) = A$ THEN GOTO 90
 80 B$ = B$ + MID$(Q$,J,1)
 90 NEXT J
100 PRINT B$
```

Line 30 is included to deal with entries of more than one character for A$. Line 50 introduces a new concept, the Null String, which is denoted by double quotes " ". This simply empties a string. Line 50 therefore creates a string variable called B$, but leaves it empty. The loop on lines 60 to 90 goes through Q$ one character at a time checking for a match with A$. If a match is not found, the character is added to B$. Note that LEN is used to determine how many characters are in Q$.

The Spectrum BASIC does not have LEFT$, RIGHT$ or MID$ as such, but uses a technique of its own called Slicing, which fulfills the same function. This uses the form

String Name (L TO M)

which gives a string consisting of the characters from positions L to M inclusive. For example:

IF A$ = "SITTINGBOURNE"

then A$(1 TO 3) will give "SIT" and A$(4 TO 7) will give "TING". The equivalent of LEFT$(A$,N) is therefore A$(1 TO N), the equivalent of MID$$*$,N,M) is A$(N TO N + M), and the equivalent of RIGHT$(A$,N) is A$(LEN(A$)−N+1 TO) because the end of the string is assumed if no number is given after TO.

A unique feature of the Sinclair string handling is the ability to modify parts of a string directly. For example:

```
10 LET A$ = "PRAGMATIC"
20 LET B$ = "AUTO"
30 LET A$(1 TO 4) = B$
40 PRINT A$
```

will give the result AUTOMATIC.

There are other string functions, but LEN, VAL, LEFT$, RIGHT$ and MID$ meet most requirements. Once these are clearly understood, the user should be able to follow the more esoteric functions.

Arrays

Let us suppose that we want to write a program to hold and display phone numbers for ten people (once we have established a principle we can extend it to any number of people).

For each entry in the telephone directory we will need to hold a name and telephone number (as an aside, we will need to hold both name and number as strings, because a number such as 02278060 would be treated as 2278060 if held as a number in a real or integer variable). One way to do this would be to allocate a list of variables as below:

Name	Phone number
N1$	P1$
N2$	P2$
N3$	P3$

and so on. If the seventh entry was, say, Smith John, with phone number 06348071, then:

    N7$ = "Smith,John"
and P7$ = "06348071"

The directory program will need to have two parts: one to enter/edit the data, and one to give phone numbers for names and vice versa. Let us just consider the problem of searching for the phone number corresponding to a name. For simplicity let us assume that the names have already been entered into N1$ to N10$, and the numbers into P1$ to P10$.

A program to find the phone number from a name could be:

```
500 INPUT "NAME"; Q$
510 TEST = −1
520 IF Q$ = N1$ THEN PRINT P1$: TEST = 1
530 IF Q$ = N2$ THEN PRINT P2$: TEST = 1
     ↓ 7 instructions 540–610
620 IF Q$ = N10$ THEN PRINT P10S: TEST = 1
630 IF TEST < 0 THEN PRINT "SORRY ";Q$;" IS NOT IN DIRECTORY"
640 GOTO 500
```

The program is quite simple; each entry is tested in turn against Q$. The variable TEST is used to record if a match is found and cause the apology on line 630 to be displayed. Note that on lines 520 to 620 each TEST = 1 is conditional on the IF at the start of the line.

Although the above program would work, it is unreasonably laborious, and would be impossible with, say, a hundred entries. What is needed is some way to store a list of similar items, and a way to access directly any specified item in the list. In BASIC this is provided by arrays.

An array is a list of items with a common name. To use an array we must first say what size of array we need. This is done with the keyword DIM (for dimension). For example:

DIM NAME$(25)

creates an array of 26 string variables (numbered from 0 to 25), all called NAME$, numbered from NAME$(0) TO NAME$(25). To find the item 7, for example, we would refer to NAME$(7). Note that array numbering starts, slightly confusingly, at zero.

DIM AGE(15)

creates an array of 16 real variables (numbered 0 to 15); AGE(9), for example, refers to item 9 in the array called AGE.

Arrays are the obvious solution to our phone directory problem. We require two arrays. N$( ) to hold the name and P$( ) to hold the corresponding phone number. If, as before, the 7th entry was "Smith,John" with phone number "06348071", then

N$(7) = "Smith, John"
P$(7) = "06348071"

The problem of finding a number from a name now becomes a simple FOR/NEXT Loop:

```
500 INPUT "NAME"; Q$
510 TEST = −1
520 FOR J% = 1 TO 10
530 IF Q$=N$(J%) THEN PRINT P$(J%): TEST = 1
540 NEXT J%
550 IF TEST < 0 THEN PRINT "SORRY ";Q$;" NOT FOUND"
560 GOTO 500
```

Note that this program would be exactly the same length regardless of how many phone numbers are held. The only difference, for say 1500 numbers, would be line 520 which would read FOR J% = 1 TO 1500 (and elsewhere the size of the two arrays would be set to 1500 in the DIM instruction).

Inputting data to an array can be done from the keyboard using INPUT (as below) or via the keywords READ, DATA described in the next section.

As an example of entering data with INPUT, the program portion below takes in pupils' names and exam marks:

```
 10 DIM N$(40),M(40)
 20 INPUT "HOW MANY PUPILS";N
 30 IF N < =40 THEN GOTO 60
 40 PRINT "SORRY, 40 IS MAXIMUM"
 50 GOTO 20
 60 FOR J% = 1 TO N
 70 PRINT "PUPIL ";J%
 80 INPUT "NAME ";N$(J%)
 90 INPUT "MARK ";M(J%)
100 INPUT "CONFIRM OK";Q$
110 IF LEFT$(Q$,1) <> "Y" THEN GOTO 70
120 NEXT J%
```

Note that lines 100/110 allow an incorrect entry to be re-entered.

As an aside, the Spectrum handles string arrays in a unique way. The DIM instruction for string arrays specifies not only the number of items in each array, but also the maximum length of each string, for example:

DIM HORSE$(8,12)

creates 8 strings (with common name HORSE$) each of length 12. Strings placed into a string array are truncated to the DIM length (if too long) or padded out with trailing spaces (if too short). With this exception, arrays on the Spectrum are used as above. PRINT HORSE$(6), for example, would print the text in the sixth variable in the array HORSE$.

READ/DATA

Often data in an array is permanently fixed. In the example below, the number of days in a month are held in an array D( ) and an abbreviated form of month name in an array M$( ). February, for example, would be represented by:

```
D(2) = 28     (ignoring leap years!)
M$(2) = "FEB"
```

These arrays will be fixed each time the program using them is run, but will need to be set up. One way to do this would be laboriously using LET:

```
100 LET D(1) = 31
110 LET M(1) = "JAN"
```

and so on for 24 instructions.

This is tedious, but fortunately BASIC allows a simpler way using the keywords READ/DATA. READ acts in a similar manner to INPUT, but the data is obtained from a list of DATA items inside the program itself. For example:

```
10 DIM D(12), M$(12)
20 FOR J% = 1TO 12
30 READ D(J%)
40 READ M$(J%)
50 NEXT J%
60 DATA 31,"JAN", 28,"FEB", 31,"MAR", 30,"APR"
70 DATA 31,"MAY", 30,"JUN", 31,"JUL", 31,"AUG"
80 DATA 30,"SEP", 31,"OCT", 30,"NOV", 31,"DEC"
```

The READ instruction starts at the first data item, 31, and puts it into D(1), then continues on with "JAN" into M$(1) until they reach "DEC" which is put into M$(12). It is obvious that the number (and position) of the DATA items and the READ instructions that use them must match. This is the programmer's responsibility; the machine cannot do it by itself.

Once read, data items cannot be read again directly. If the RESTORE keyword is used, however, the next READ will be made from the first DATA item in the program again (and subsequent READs in sequence from the first again). DATA items can be put anywhere in the program but it is good practice to put them either after the READ instruction that uses them or at the end of the program.

Multi-dimension arrays

The arrays we have dealt with so far are called single-dimension arrays. Arrays can, however, be multi-dimensional. The horse names for eight races (each with 10

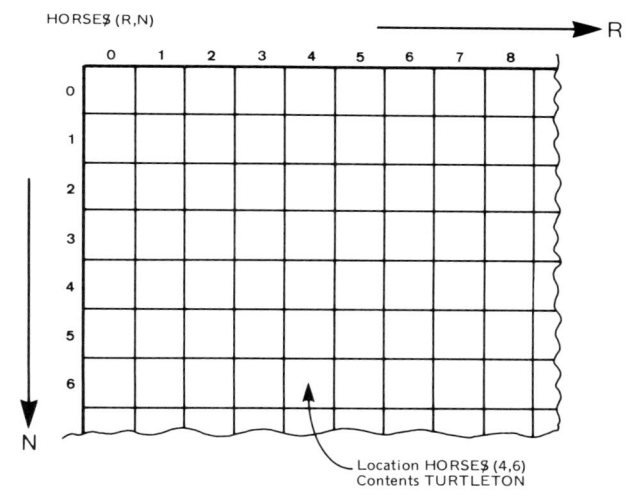

Figure 3.8. A multidimensional array

horses), for example, could be held in a single two dimension array:

HORSE$(R,N)

where R is the race number and N the horse number. If the sixth horse in the fourth race was called "TURTLETON", then:

HORSE$(4,6) = "TURTLETON"

The array can be visualised as Figure 3.8.

Multi-dimensional arrays use a lot of store space, particularly for strings.

Functions

Functions are used by BASIC where some form of result is to be calculated. A value, either direct from a variable or an expression, is used by a function to give the required result.

A typical function, available in most BASICs, is SQR which is used to give square roots. For example:

    Y = SQR(16)

will give variable Y the value 4.

The simple program:

    10 FOR J = 1 TO 10
    20 PRINT SQR(J)
    30 NEXT J

will print out a table of the square roots of the numbers 1 to 10. Similarly the program below gives the hypotenuse of a right angle triangle given the other two sides:

    10 INPUT "FIRST SIDE ";A
    20 INPUT "SECOND SIDE ";B
    30 PRINT "HYPOTENUSE IS ";SQR(A*A + B*B)

SQR is a typical function; the input value (direct, from a variable or an expression) is enclosed in brackets after the function name.

BASIC provides many functions, but as this chapter does not intend to be an exhaustive guide it would be a bit space-consuming to list them all. Some of the more common are given below. All operate on numbers, values of variables and expressions.

INT (for integer) rounds a value *down*. INT(2.472) is therefore 2, INT(27.98) is 27. If it is required to round to the nearest whole number, 0.5 should be added to the value to be operated on by INT. For example INT(X + 0.5) will round the value of variable X to the nearest whole number. INT can also be used to round to any required places of decimals by multiplying by powers of ten before using INT, then dividing the INT value by the same power of ten. For example:

    (INT(100*NUM + 0.5))/100

will give NUM rounded to two places of decimal. If NUM had the value 8.24512, the above expression would give the result 8.25.

Related to INT is ABS. This gives the magnitude of a value (i.e. the sign of the result is always positive):

ABS (5.429) is 5.429
ABS (−2.197) is 2.197

Trigonometrical functions SIN, COS, TAN are provided in all but the simplest BASICs, and the inverse functions (ASN, ACS, ATN) in some. These will mainly be of interest to people who know what SIN, COS, TAN mean! It should be noted that these operate in radians (to convert from degrees to radians, multiply by 3.141592 and divide by 180. A radian is about 57 degrees. Some BASICs provide functions RAD and DEG to provide the conversion).

Other mathematical functions are EXP (the mathematical number e raised to a specified power). LN (logarithms to base e), LOG (logarithms to base ten). Again these will only be of interest to people who know what they mean mathematically.

Functions can operate directly on functions. For example:

INT (SQR(10))

will give the value 3.

An expression operated on by a function can be any desired complexity. For example:

R = INT(A*COS(SQR (B*B+1))+ C*EXP(INT(D)))

is a perfectly valid instruction using five functions.

Most BASICs allow the programmer to define his own functions using the keyword DEFN. This is not described here as this is felt to be beyond the remit of an introductory book. Full details of DEFN are given in *Beginner's Guide to BASIC Programming*.

Random numbers

Games (and simulations) require random numbers. A backgammon game, for example, requires two dice which are effectively two random numbers in the range 1–6. All BASICs give random numbers with the function RND, although there are slight variations on the way different machines use it.

Some generate a number in the range 0 to 0.999999 (to how many significant figures the machine uses). It can take the value 0, but not 1. The Spectrum, for example, uses this technique. The simple program:

```
10 FOR J = 1 TO 5
20 PRINT RND
30 NEXT J
```

could give the result

```
0.996322632
0.147295134
0.426179258
0.008357826
0.497026638
```

Integer numbers (for dice for example) are obtained by multiplying the value given by RND:

INT (6*RND)

will give random numbers in the range 0 to 5, so 1 + INT(6*RND) will give random numbers 1 to 6 for dice.

The second approach uses the form RND(N) which gives an integer in the range 1 to N *inclusive*. The program below therefore simulates rolling a dice four times:

```
10 FOR J = 1 TO 4
20 PRINT RND(6)
30 NEXT J
```

A typical display could be:

```
3
1
6
2
```

Some machines (such as the BBC) support both forms; RND(1) behaving like the Spectrum RND and RND(N) where N is positive and not 1 giving numbers in the range 1 to N.

Random numbers from RND are, in reality, a pseudo-random sequence of over 65 000 numbers. Using the keyword RANDOMIZE it is possible to force a program to start at a specific point in the sequence (which is useful in simulations where different strategies are to be tested) or at a random point (for games). Usually:

RANDOMIZE N starts at the Nth number
RANDOMIZE starts at a random point

Some machines (again the BBC for example) use a negative number with RND (e.g. RND(−5)) to give the same effect as RANDOMIZE.

Conclusion

BASIC is an ideal language for the beginner, but the user should not attempt to learn every function and keyword. This chapter has aimed to describe what is needed to get started rather than give rigorous definitions. The reader should now be able to read the BASIC manual for a specific machine with understanding.

Chapter 4 will build on this foundation and describe programming techniques and languages other than BASIC.

4

Not-so-BASIC programming

Bloody instructions, which, being taught, return
To plague the inventor.

Shakespeare

Introduction

The previous chapter provided a grounding in BASIC, the language provided with almost all microcomputers (the one notable exception, the Jupiter ACE which used FORTH, ceased production late in 1983). This chapter delves further into the art of programming, starting with the steps involved in writing a program and getting it to work (de-bugging in the jargon). Later sections cover topics such as good style, structured programming and other languages (including machine code).

Writing programs

Someone once wrote that he was sure that designing a suspension bridge was easy, if only he knew where to start. In many respects writing a program is similar; the hardest step is the first.

The novice should not be over-ambitious; too many people try to write a complex arcade game (with fast-moving graphics and intricate sound) as their first program. Not surprisingly, most fail and many become disheartened and convinced that programming is difficult. It is essential, therefore, to learn to walk before trying to run. If your interest is arcade-type games, experiment with moving shapes around the screen, explore the sound capabilities of your machine by writing a simple music program. Work up to the full game in stages. Similarly, do not try to write a program to do the accounts for a small business in one go.

The first stage in writing a reasonable-sized program is to define what it is to do. This is known, rather grandly, as 'systems analysis' and should be given at least as much (if not

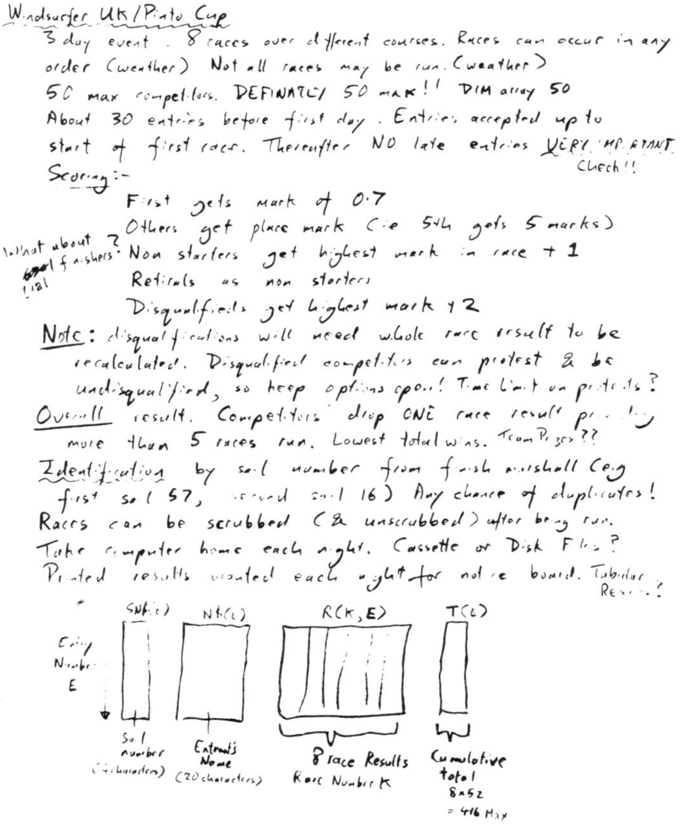

Handwritten notes:

Windsurfer UK/Pinto Cup
3 day event. 8 races over different courses. Races can occur in any order (weather) Not all races may be run. (weather)
50 max competitors. DEFINATELY 50 max!! DIM array 50
About 30 entries before first day. Entries accepted up to start of first race. Thereafter NO late entries VERY IMPORTANT
Scoring:—   Check!!
        First gets mark of 0.7
        Others get place mark (ie 5th gets 5 marks)
What about? Non starters get highest mark in race + 1
equal finishers Retirals as non starters
        Disqualifieds get highest mark + 2
Note: disqualifications will need whole race result to be recalculated. Disqualified competitors can protest & be undisqualified, so keep options open! Time limit on protests?
Overall result. Competitors drop ONE race result probably more than 5 races run. Lowest total wins. Team Prizes??
Identification by sail number from finish marshall (e.g. first sail 57, second sail 16) Any chance of duplicates!
Races can be scrubbed (& unscrubbed) after being run.
Take computer home each night. Cassette or Disk Files?
Printed results wanted each night for notice board. Tabular Results!

SN(i)   NN(i)   R(k,E)   T(i)

Entry Number E

Sail number (4 character)   Entrant's Name (20 characters)   8 race Results Race Number k   Cumulative total 8×52 = 416 Max

Figure 4.1. First stage notes for a program

103

more) time as the actual writing of the program. At this stage, all the awkward 'What happens if?' questions should be asked. Recently the author was involved in using a computer to work out the results of a three-day windsurfing competition. Figure 4.1 shows some notes made at an early stage of the design and show the sort of detail required and the questions to be asked before a single instruction is written. In a games program, the 'plot', key operations, video displays, scoring etc., should all be clearly defined at this stage.

The analysis of the requirements of programs for business is particularly important, as an unexpected set of circumstances arising when the program has been in service for some months can be catastrophic. The importance of the analysis stage cannot be overemphasized; it is not possible to write a good program if you do not understand what it is supposed to do!

The next stage is to break the program down, as far as possible, into small 'tasks' or sub-programs. This has several advantages, not least of which is the fact that it makes the whole thing more manageable. In the jargon this is known as 'top-down programming', because you start with a job to be done, which is broken down into smaller jobs, which can themselves be broken down into yet smaller tasks and so on as shown in Figure 4.2.

If possible, these small tasks should be chosen so they are capable of being written and tested outside of other tasks and the main program. In the windsurfer race example earlier, for example, one small task was finding a competitor's name and race number given the sail number, all of which were held in multi-dimensional arrays. This task was written on its own then combined with a small test program which set up a dummy array with competitor 1 having sail number 0101 and name AA and so on to competitor 50 with sail number 5050 and name BX. With this dummy array, it was easy to test the 'Find details from Sail number' task before it became part of a larger (and harder to understand) program.

Typical small tasks in a games program could be 'Read keyboard', 'Move man', 'Spaceship explodes' and so on. Sub

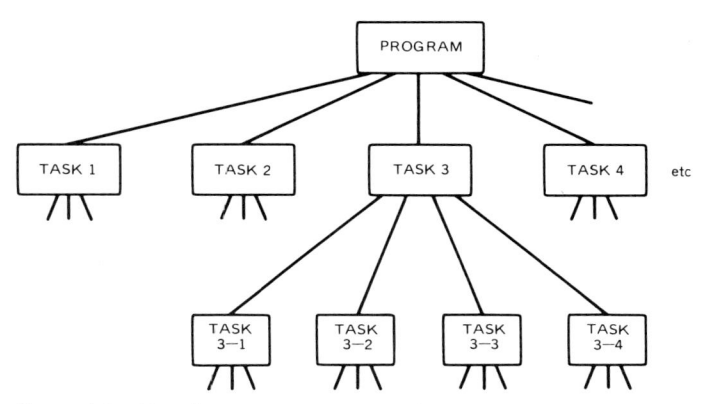

Figure 4.2. Top-down programming with tasks and sub-tasks

tasks of 'Spaceship explodes' could be 'Explosion display' and 'Explosion sounds', both of which would be a task of relatively few instructions which could be tested on its own.

During planning, it helps if each task is allocated a range of line numbers in the main program at the Figure 4.2 stage, and the identity (i.e. the variable names) of data passing between the tasks established. In the 'Find details from Sail Number' task above, for example, the variable name SN% was chosen

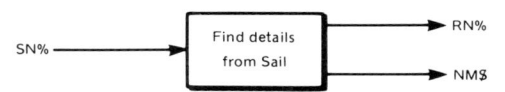

Figure 4.3. Representation of a sub task

to pass the sail number to the task, which then put the corresponding competitor's race number into the variable RN% and the name into the string variable NM$. The task could therefore be represented by Figure 4.3.

The small tasks themselves (and the linking of the small tasks to form a complete program) are best described via flowcharts, which are easy-to-follow visual representations of a programs operation.

There are five symbols required for drawing a flow chart. There are no real standards, but the symbols for Figure 4.4 are widely used.

1. Input denotes input of data (usually from the keyboard).
2. Output denotes output of data (to TV screen or printer).
3. Operation can denote any manipulation of data, from a single instruction to an entire task.

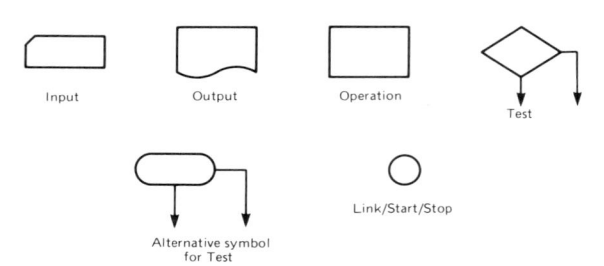

Figure 4.4. Common flow-chart symbols

4. Test (usually based on an IF instruction). Unlike other symbols this has more than one output route dependent on the test on the symbol. The output routes should be labelled, e.g. Yes, No.
5. Link/Start/Stop. This symbol shows the start and finish of a flow chart. These can obviously be the true Start/Stop of a program or links to other flowcharts. Links are usually labelled with a letter (A, B, C etc.) to make the links easy to follow (Link A in task 7, for example, goes to Link A on flow chart 23).

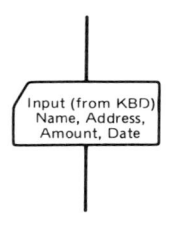

Figure 4.5. Flow-chart symbol covering several instructions

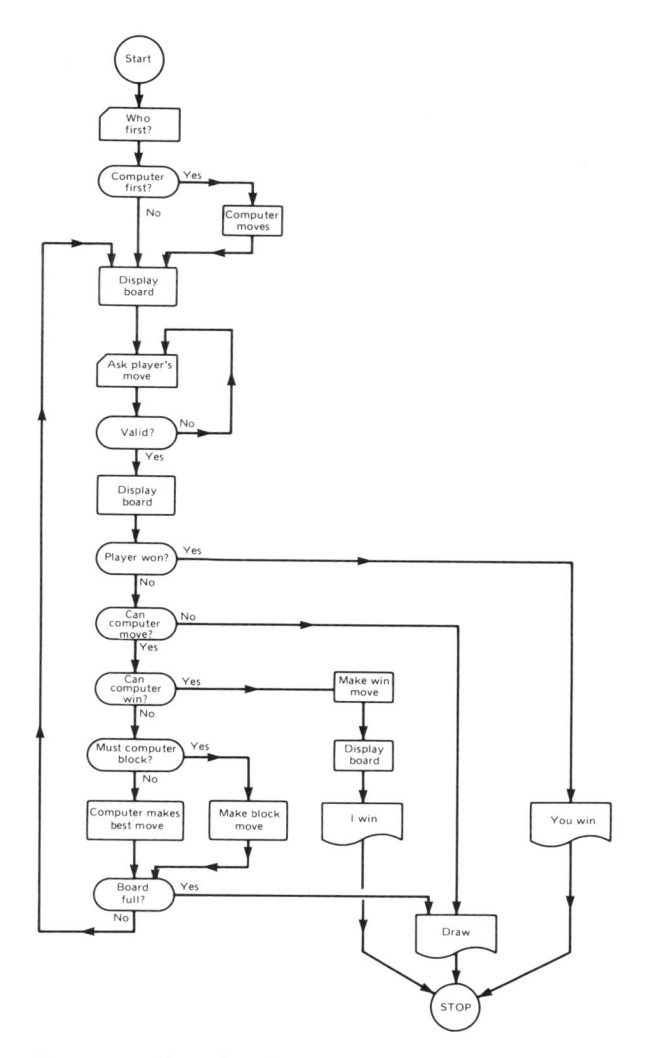

Figure 4.6. Flow chart for noughts and crosses program

It is not necessary for each symbol to correspond to one and only one instruction. If, say, we were showing the input of a customer's name, address, amount paid, and date, this would all be done with one symbol as in Figure 4.5. Similarly Figure 4.6 shows a flow chart for a program to enable a computer to play noughts and crosses. Note that this simply shows the flow of the program and identifies likely sub tasks (Computer Makes Best Move, Display Board; the latter is an obvious candidate for a subroutine as it occurs three times).

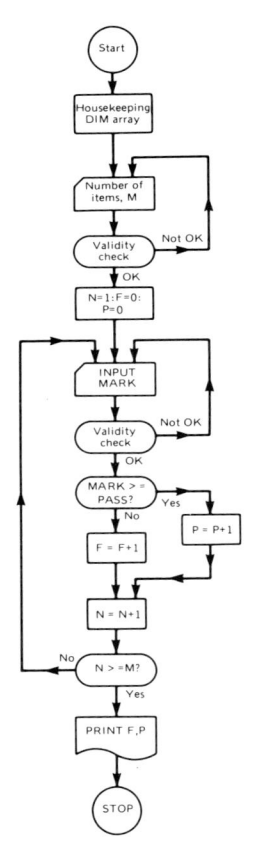

Figure 4.7. Flow chart which can be converted directly to program instructions

Figure 4.7, however, is a flow chart for a sub task where each box corresponds more or less directly with a BASIC instruction. This sub task inputs exam marks and totals passes and fails. Variable M holds the number of marks, variable F holds the number of fails and variable P the number of passes. A complete sub task could be written from Figure 4.7 without the need for a more detailed flow chart.

Algorithms

Figure 4.6 shows a flow chart for a noughts and crosses program, which includes a few enigmatic boxes such as 'Computer Makes Best Move', without describing how it does this.

Expanding this box requires knowledge on behalf of the programmer; it is not possible to write a game programme without knowing how to evaluate the optimum move. This again emphasises the need for a clear understanding of the use to which a program is to be put.

The rules and strategy for arriving at a solution are called an 'Algorithm' in the jargon. There is no general rule for deriving algorithms; they depend largely on the programmer's experience and general knowledge. The place to start for the noughts and crosses program, for example, would be a book on games strategy from the local library, or simply to play the game with pencil and paper and try to identify the best moves.

All the commonly needed algorithms (such as sorts) are well documented in computer books and magazines, and one of the most useful things an aspiring programmer can do is examine the literature and build up a library of useful algorithms.

The so-called Bubble Sort is a simple common algorithm, which is used to put a list of items in order (e.g. Scores, Names and so on). The Bubble Sort, loosely described, keeps going through the list swapping items that need exchanging until it goes through the list and finds none need swapping.

For example, suppose we are going to sort the four numbers 5,1,7,2 with the highest to the left. We start:

- a. 5 1 7 2   Compare 5,1 correct
- b. 5 1 7 2   Compare 1,7 (next items), incorrect, swap them
- c. 5 7 1 2   Compare 1,2 incorrect, swap them
- d. 5 7 2 1   Last pair, start again. Compare 5,7 incorrect swap them
- e. 7 5 2 1   Compare 5,2 correct
- f. 7 5 2 1   Compare 2,1 correct
- g. 7 5 2 1   Last pair, start again. Compare 7,5 correct
- h. 7 5 2 1   Compare 5,2 correct
- i. 7 5 2 1   Compare 2,1 correct

We have been right through the list (steps g–i) without needing to make a swap, so the list is sorted. Note that the list was actually correct at step e, but we needed further steps to make sure that no further swaps were needed.

Although this is very tedious to perform by hand, it is ideally suited for a computer. More rigorously, the algorithm can be expressed:

1. Set Marker = 0 (This is a variable that records when a swap has been made.)
2. Go through list comparing adjacent pairs. If a pair is in the wrong order, swap them and make Marker = 1.
3. If at the end of the list, Marker = 1 go back to step a. If Marker = 0 (indicating no swaps were made on last pass) then list is sorted.

This algorithm is shown in flow chart form in Figure 4.8.

Menu-driven programs

Many programs can conveniently be constructed as a Menu of options for the user. The Windsurfing race example earlier, for example, had the menu:

Options are: 1. Enter/Modify Entrant's Details
                2. View Entrant's Details/Marks
                3. Enter/Modify Race Result

4. Scratch/Reinstate Race
5. Print Entrant List
6. Print Interim/Final Result
7. Backup Storage Save/Load

Enter Option Number ?

The user enters the required option number and the computer reacts accordingly.

Menu-driven programs have the form of Figure 4.9, and have many advantages for the programmer. In particular, they are very easy to 'debug' because once the central display and option selection task is working the option tasks can be written and tested one at a time.

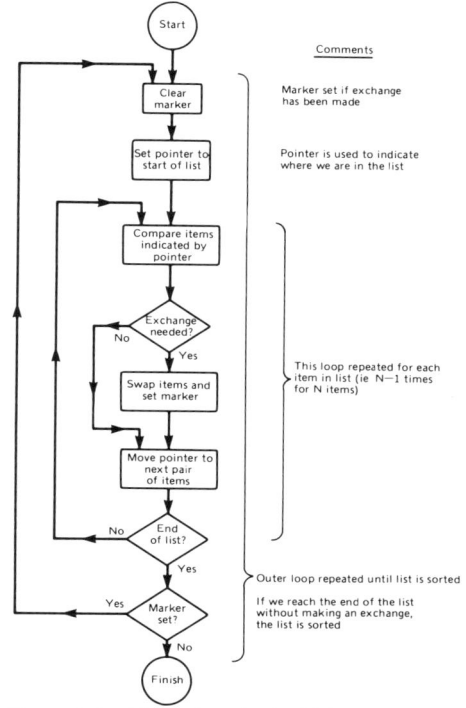

Figure 4.8. Flow chart for bubble sort

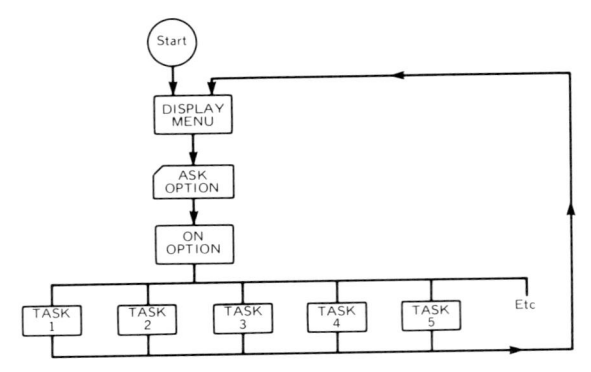

Figure 4.9. Flow chart of a menu-driven program

Menu-driven programs are also easy to modify. The addition of an option simply requires a small change to the central menu program and the addition of another task to meet the option needs. A called task can itself, of course, have a menu (one option of which returns to the main menu).

Programming for speed

Speed is not normally a problem, but BASIC is not the fastest of computer languages, and there are times when a program needs every ounce of speed (arcade games for example). The guidelines below will give a significant increase in speed. Unfortunately some of them destroy the comprehensibility of a program, but speed and ease of reading are incompatible.

1. Leave out all REM lines (but check that no other instruction has a GOTO or GOSUB to the line you are omitting).
2. Use integer variables wherever possible, and keep variable names short.
3. Use multiple instruction lines;

    1000 FOR I% = 1 TO 100 : D(I%) = 0 : NEXT I%

runs faster than:

```
1000 FOR I% = 1 TO 100
1010 D(I%) = 0
1020 NEXT I%
```

4. Do not have redundant instructions in a loop. For example, in

```
1500 FOR J% = 1 TO 100
1510 P = 219.25
1520 A(J%) = P*J%*B%(J%)
1530 NEXT J%
```

the instruction P = 219.25 is being obeyed unnecessarily some 99 times. Instruction 1510 is redundant, and variable P should have been set to 219.25 just before the loop. Although this fault is obvious, such redundant instructions are common.

5. Avoid GOTOs if possible, particularly in loops, FOR/NEXT is quicker.
6. Use defined functions (DEFFN) wherever possible rather than GOSUB. Some BASICs (notably BBC) use PROCEDUREs which are also quicker than GOSUBs.
7. Some BASICs allow the control variable to be omitted after NEXT (e.g. FOR I% = 1 TO 10 : PRINT I% : NEXT). This often gives a small improvement in speed.
8. Avoid functions like SIN, COS, TAN, SQR etc. Also remember that addition/subtraction is faster than multiplication and division which is faster than raising to the power, so A + A is faster than 2*A; A*A*A is faster than A ↑ 3. If the more complex functions are needed to no great accuracy a look-up table can be set up in an array, which is initially loaded at the start of a program. A = S(X) is then a lot faster than A = SQR(X), for example.
9. BASIC gets numbers faster from a variable than from a constant, so loops in particular can be speeded up by assigning variables to any constant used thereafter. For example

```
500 LET Z% = 32 : LET FC = 5/9
510 FOR F% = 0 TO 212
520 LET C(F%) = (F% - Z%)*FC
530 NEXT F%
```

will operate much faster than:

```
500 FOR F% = 0 TO 212
510 LET C(F%) = (F% - 32)*5/9
520 NEXT F%
```

even though it has one extra line. Actually, in both programs using 0.55556 is faster than using 5/9.
10. In some BASICs, instructions near the front of a program operate faster than those at the end. This feature can be used to advantage.
11. Keep the programs as short as possible; omit all unnecessary spaces.
12. Examine the literature for fast ways of doing things, a so called Shell Sort is four times faster than the Bubble Sort of Figure 4.8; there are at least four different ways of drawing a circle on the TV screen, each with its own advantages.

Following the above steps should give a significant increase in speed, but for really high speed it is necessary to use a Compiler or Machine Code; topics we shall return to later.

Debugging a program

Very few programs work correctly first time; most have several faults in them when written. Faults in a program are known as bugs; finding and correcting these faults is inevitably known as debugging. There are generally two types of bugs: grammatical errors (usually caused by typing mistakes) and logical errors (which cause a program to behave in an unexpected manner).

Typing and grammatical errors will usually bring up some form of error message from the computer (e.g. NEXT without FOR at line 150, or NO SUCH VARIABLE at line 1370). These error messages do not always indicate the line at which the true error occurs. A NEXT without FOR error at line 150 could mean the FOR instruction at an earlier line has been omitted. The NO SUCH VARIABLE at line 1370 could mean that a LET instruction on an earlier line was mistyped. Similarly a NO SUCH LINE error message on a GOTO instruction (e.g. GOTO 250) could mean that the number after the GOTO is incorrect, or the line number of the GOTO target instruction has been incorrectly entered.

Most error messages are, however, self-explanatory. Missing brackets, commas and quotes are very common. Extra spaces can also sometimes cause trouble; although BASIC is very tolerant of spaces in general, some machines will object to GO TO or TAB (11,15). Some machines have their own quirks; TANDY BASIC, for example, uses PRINT @, but the @ must be entered in lower case. Unfortunately shifted @ looks just the same on the screen, but the computer says Syntax Error on an apparently correct line. The moral is: if in doubt, retype the whole line carefully.

Most machines only check lines for syntax when the program is run. The Sinclair machines (Spectrum and ZX81) check syntax as each line is entered which helps to pick up a lot of typing errors. There is, however, still no protection against incorrect line numbers in GOTOs or GOSUBs or typing errors such as entering letter I for numeral 1, letter O for numeral 0 (and vice versa) or mistyped variable names.

With the program grammatically correct, there is still no guarantee that it will run. Logical errors are mistakes made by the programmer, and these can often be difficult to find because during the checking there is a tendency to see what you expect to see.

There are many common logical errors. One is known as the plus or minus one syndrome, which is typified by the question 'How many days are there between Monday and Saturday?'. Dependent on circumstances, the answer can be 4, 5 or 6. If care is not taken, loops can operate one time too few or one time too many.

A similar error can occur because FOR/NEXT loops always execute at least once. If, for example, we have:

```
650 FOR J = 1 TO MAX
    Instructions
700 NEXT J
```

Where MAX is a variable, the loop will be executed once for all values of MAX less than two. This is probably not what the programmer intended. More sophisticated languages than BASIC have a similar instruction DO WHILE/END which does not have this undesirable characteristic.

A very common (and elusive) error is caused by using the same variable name for two different purposes. A typical error, shown in Figure 4.10, uses the same variable for a loop counter in the main program and in a subroutine called

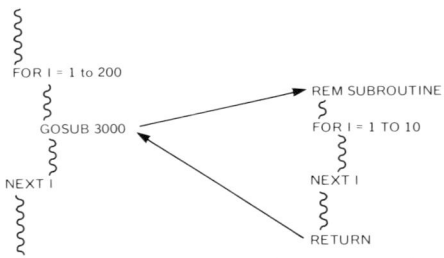

```
FOR I = 1 to 200                    REM SUBROUTINE
    GOSUB 3000                      FOR I = 1 TO 10
NEXT I                              NEXT I
                                    RETURN
```

Figure 4.10. A common bug; using the same variable twice

inside the main program loop. Figure 4.10 would, in fact, cause the program to loop indefinitely and would not give any error messages. It is very important to keep a record of variable names and where they are used to avoid this sort of clash.

A problem which make take some time to show is the Unexpected Condition. This is typified by some input combination which the programmer did not expect, or by some requirement that was overlooked. Often these show up as a 'Division by Zero' error message, and are best avoided by careful thought at the Systems Analysis stage. Programs should always be tested thoroughly to make sure that unexpected data entry of (say) zero does not cause the program to crash.

One of the most useful debugging weapons is the STOP instruction. The value of a variable is not cleared when a program terminates, and can be examined directly in the same way as we saw earlier when the machine was used as a calculator. For example, suppose we have the simple program:

```
10 FOR I = 1 TO 4
20 A = 3.12*I
30 PRINT I
40 NEXT I
```

When run, this would give:

```
1
2
3
4
```

and finish. The variables A and I still exist, however, as we can see by typing:

```
PRINT I
     5
PRINT A
     12.48
```

(Note that I is one greater than the loop limit for reason explained in the previous chapter.)

Temporary STOP instructions can be inserted at strategic points in the program to show where it is going. Values of variables can then be examined using direct PRINT instructions. The execution of the program can be continued by entering directly a GOTO the line number after the stop instruction. This can only be done if no modifications are made whilst the program is not running. Any changes to the program will cause all variables to be cleared.

It cannot be overemphasized that debugging is easiest on programs that are logically constructed in sub tasks as outlined earlier. A straggly, illconceived program is likely to contain bugs, and these bugs will be difficult to find in the spaghetti.

Programming style

A good program should:

(a) Work correctly under all circumstances.
(b) Be simple to use and 'friendly' to the user.
(c) Written in such a way that its operation is obvious.
(d) Be easy to debug.
(e) Be easy to modify.

Most beginners consider only the first aspect, and it could be argued that a working program is all that is required. However, anyone who is aiming to write programs for use by other people should consider all the items above to be of equal importance.

User input and displays are often overlooked. Good checking of user input data is essential (called 'Validation' in the jargon). Care should be taken to ensure that the format of inputs is consistent and is the form normally encountered by the user. A program for, say, stock control which asks for 'Bin Number, Item, Quantity' in part of the program and 'Item, Bin Number, Quantity' somewhere else, with other paper work in the firm being arranged 'Quantity, Item, Bin Number' is asking for trouble.

Particular care should be taken where entries can be confused. The author has seen a particularly bad example where a computer was used to cut steel bars. These were identified by a 4 digit length (in mm) and a 4 digit quality identifier. Inevitably, a whole shift was cut to a length of 3927 with quality 4200 instead of a length of 4200 and code 3927. Beware of such possibilities; remember Murphy's Law that anything that *can* go wrong *will* go wrong.

Displays should be clear and uncluttered. Always aim to work on a simple fixed display (i.e. do not scroll the screen like paper from a typewriter). If the user is entering data from some type of form, aim to put the data on the screen roughly in the same place as it appears on the form. Avoid flashing characters, spectacular graphics (except in games) and jokey comments. These all amuse for a short time, but rapidly become tedious and even annoying.

Items (c), (d) and (e) are all really linked, and come down to the way in which a program is written. The idea of tasks and subtasks outlined earlier (called modular programming) leads to a program which is easy to follow and modify.

Academics refer to structured programs. It can be shown that any program can be written with just the first four forms of Figure 4.11. An operation is obvious, it can be anything from a single instruction to a full task. Loops are constructed with two structures: Do While (condition) in which the test precedes the operation, the Repeat Until (condition) where

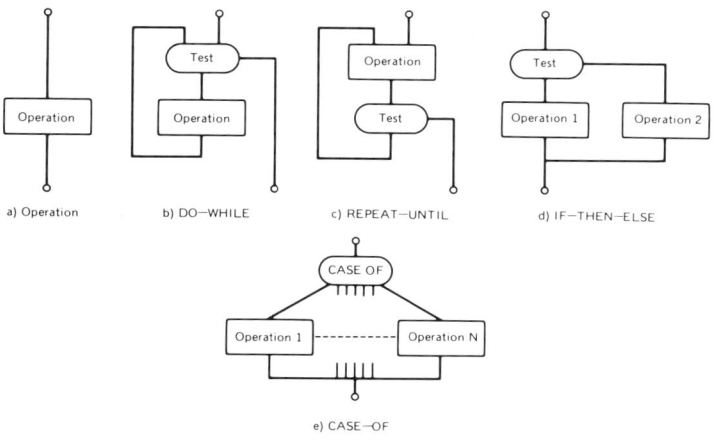

a) Operation   b) DO—WHILE   c) REPEAT—UNTIL   d) IF—THEN—ELSE

e) CASE—OF

Figure 4.11. Structured programming

the operation precedes the test. Note that with Repeat Until the operation is performed at least once. The final form, IF . . . . THEN . . . ELSE, is used for alternative operations based on a test. Sometimes the CASE OF form (Figure 4.11e) is included in the basic structures, but it is not really essential.

A program written in the form of the building blocks of Figure 4.11 is said to be 'structured', and will, of necessity, be written in a top-down manner as described earlier. One of the features of a structured program is that it appears as a straightforward line, and cannot degenerate into a bird's nest of GOTOs.

Another feature of structured programs is the use of procedures and user-defined functions. These are superficially similar to subroutines, but are called by name rather than line number. Functions are used where a single result is to be returned, procedures for all other operations.

A structured program written using procedures and functions consists of a short main program which is mainly procedure and function calls followed by the actual procedure and function definitions. For example, the main program for the noughts and crosses example of Figure 4.6 simplifies to:

```
PROCwhofirst
IF computerfirst THEN PROCcomputermove
REPEAT
    PROCgame
UNTIL FNcomplete
PROCresult
```

This is not written in any particular language, but rather in a 'pseudo code' used for planning programs. PROC is a call to a named procedure, computerfirst is a Boolean variable, and FNcomplete a function which looks at the state of the board and returns a Value that can again only be TRUE or FALSE.

This would be followed by all the procedure and function definitions. PROCgame, for example, becomes:

```
DEFPROCgame
  PROCdisplay
  PROCplayermove
  PROCdisplay
  IF FNcomplete = FALSE THEN PROCcomputermove
ENDPROC
```

Note that this calls further procedures and functions.

It is very difficult to write structured programs in BASIC, although BBC BASIC does include REPEAT UNTIL, procedures and user-defined functions. Most BASICs just have user-defined functions, IF and FOR . . . . NEXT (which is a restricted form of REPEAT UNTIL). Academics therefore dislike BASIC, in particular its reliance on the GOTO keyword.

There is some justification for this view. A typical BASIC example (from a game called KING) is:

```
500 INPUT "HOW MANY ACRES";I
510 IF I > = 0 GOTO 530
520 GOTO 500
530 IF I > AG GOTO 580
540 J=I/2 : IF J > = S GOTO 560
550 GOSUB 1000 : GOTO 500
560 IF I > 10*P GOTO 550
570 GOTO 590
580 IF B < 0.5*RND(8) GOTO 560
590 GOTO 100
```

It works, but is it clear? easy to modify? easy to debug?

BASIC is not the only computer language, and there are several which have been written specifically to encourage structured programming. The commonest are PASCAL and COMAL (both, not surprisingly, having originated in an academic background). We shall return to other computer languages later in this chapter.

Interpreters and compilers

As we shall see later, a microcomputer (or, for that matter, any computer) understands only a very limited range of simple instructions called its Machine Code Instruction set. No microcomputer directly understands BASIC, PASCAL, FORTH, LISP or any other high-level language. Before a program can be run, therefore, it must be converted to a machine-code form that the computer itself can follow. There are two ways that this can be achieved: by an interpreter or a compiler. Simply put, an interpreter converts a high-level program written in, say, BASIC, to its machine-code equivalent an instruction at a time as it is being run. A compiler converts the whole program to machine code *before* it is run. Interpreters and compilers are, themselves, programs held in ROM or on disk in the machine itself.

Because an interpreter does the conversion as it runs, it is obviously slower. Typically a compiled program will run some five to ten times faster than the same program run under an interpreter. This is not the whole story, though. An interpreter holds the program in the form that it is originally entered (called the source program). At any time, the program can be stopped, corrections made and the program run again.

Using a compiler is far more involved. First a program called an Editor is loaded. This is similar, in principle, to the operation of a word processor, and is used to enter, and modify, the source program. With the source program in place, the actual compiler program is loaded and used to convert the source program to machine code (called the object program) which can then be run.

Correcting errors with a compiler is not simple. The source program has to be reloaded, and the editor used to make the correction. The compiler must then be used to create a totally new object program, which can be tested. A simple change which could take under a minute with an interpreter can take 15 minutes with a compiler.

A compiler, therefore, gives fast, efficient programs, but the writing and debugging can be a slow and annoying business. An interpreter runs programs slower (but adequately for most purposes) but allows corrections to be made easily and quickly. Interpreters also require less memory. Almost all microcomputers use an interpreter, because user-friendliness and memory capacity are more important than speed.

Compiled languages are available for microcomputers; PASCAL and FORTH are invariably compiled, and compilers are available for BASIC. An excellent compromise is to do the debugging with an interpreter, and when a correct program is obtained use a compiler to get a fast version. The one major drawback is that disks and a printer are needed to use a compiler to full advantage.

Programming languages

BASIC is used so extensively in microcomputers that it is natural for newcomers to assume that all computing is done in BASIC. In fact, BASIC is only one of many hundred high-level languages, each with its own advantages and peculiarities. BASIC is widely used because it is easy to learn and easy to teach (and so is particularly attractive to schools) and is somewhat a 'Jack of all trades' language; it can do most things you might want to do with a computer.

It is quite possible to use computers professionally and never use any language other than BASIC, but such a view is rather blinkered. Other computer languages are not only interesting, but can generate new insights into the way computers work. Whatever task you wish to use a computer for, it is probable that a language has been written specifically for that purpose. The aspiring programmer should aim to have at least a nodding acquaintance with other languages.

It is obviously not possible in a book of this size to give a detailed study of any computer language, let alone a survey of all. The sections below introduce some of the commoner languages which are available for microcomputers.

FORTRAN

This was one of the earliest high-level languages, and its name is an acronym for FORmula TRANslation, i.e. it is aimed at the scientific and engineering user. BASIC is actually based on FORTRAN, so the BASIC user is not likely to have problems following a FORTRAN program.

A typical small FORTRAN program is:

```
C   PROGRAM TO PRINTOUT MULTIPLICATION TABLES
    REAL TABLE,RES
    INTEGER I
C
    CALL ASSIGN(1,'TI:')
    WRITE (1,100)
    READ (1,200) TABLE
    DO 5 I = 1,10
    RES = I*TABLE
```

```
      WRITE (1,300)I,TABLE,RES
    5 CONTINUE
  100 FORMAT (1X,' WHICH TIMES TABLE?')
  200 FORMAT (F6.1)
  300 FORMAT (1X,I2,' TIMES ',F5.1,' IS ',F5.1)
      STOP
      END
```

Some of this is familiar, some probably appears odd. FORTRAN uses variable names in the same way as BASIC, but these have to be declared by REAL, INTEGER. FORTRAN also recognises LOGICAL (true and false) DOUBLE PRECISION and COMPLEX. Although some implementations of FORTRAN do provide for character manipulation, string handling is not a strong point of FORTRAN.

WRITE and READ are the equivalent of PRINT and INPUT. The instruction defines a device (terminal 1 in our example which is assigned to our terminal TI) and a line number where the form of input is to be found. Line numbers are essential only for FORMAT lines, the destination of GOTOs and the end of loops. In the FORMAT statements, text is enclosed in quotes, 1X means a new line, F5.1 denotes a fixed format number, with 5 denoting the number of digits and .1 the number of decimal places. I2 is a two-digit integer.

DO is the FORTRAN equivalent of FOR NEXT, but the loop end is denoted by a line number following DO (5 in our example). I is used as the loop counter which goes from 1 to 10.

C stands for Comment and is the FORTRAN equivalent of REM.

FORTRAN uses IF and GOTO almost identically to BASIC, although conditions such as < or > are represented by .LE. or .GT. and = by .EQ. (the = sign in a mathematical instruction means the same in FORTRAN and BASIC of course, as in SUM = A1+A2+A3).

Subroutines in FORTRAN are CALLed by name, and values are passed between main programs and subroutines in a more logical manner than BASIC uses. For example, suppose we have a simple subroutine to find the highest of two numbers. This could be defined:

```
SUBROUTINE MAX(FIRST,SECOND,BIGGEST)
BIGGEST = FIRST
IF(SECOND .GT. FIRST) BIGGEST = SECOND
RETURN
```

This subroutine can be called by:

```
CALL MAX(A,B,C)
```

with the result that the values of variables A,B will be compared and the largest value put in variable C.

FORTRAN is always compiled, but is available for most microcomputers equipped with disk drives. Its similarity to BASIC makes it a good choice as a first alternative language, but its lack of structure (which it shares with BASIC) does not appeal to academics.

LOGO

This language was conceived as a computer language for primary school children by the academic Seymour Papert. Although it does exist as a complete language in its own right, what is usually provided under the name 'LOGO' is the excellent picture-drawing facilities known as 'Turtle Graphics'. These introduce very young children to the idea of programming a computer, and allow very complex patterns to be displayed with very few instructions.

In Turtle Graphics a small triangle on the screen simulates a remote-control vehicle which can be driven around by commands such as Forward, Left, Right and so on. Distances are measured in arbitrary units (typically 1000 from top to bottom and side to side) and angles in degrees. The triangle is known as a 'Turtle'. As the turtle moves, it leaves a trail on the screen. Instructions such as PENUP, PENDOWN, COLOUR allow the trail to be inhibited or drawn in a different colour. The commands

```
FORWARD 200
RIGHT 90
FORWARD 200
```

would therefore produce the display of Figure 4.12.

The word REPEAT followed by a number is the equivalent of a FOR NEXT loop, so

REPEAT 4, FORWARD 100 : RIGHT 90

would draw a square, the forward and right instructions being repeated four times.

Variable names are used as in BASIC, but the keyword is MAKE rather than LET. For example:

MAKE EDGE = 200
REPEAT 4, FORWARD EDGE : RIGHT 90

will draw a square of side EDGE (i.e. 200).

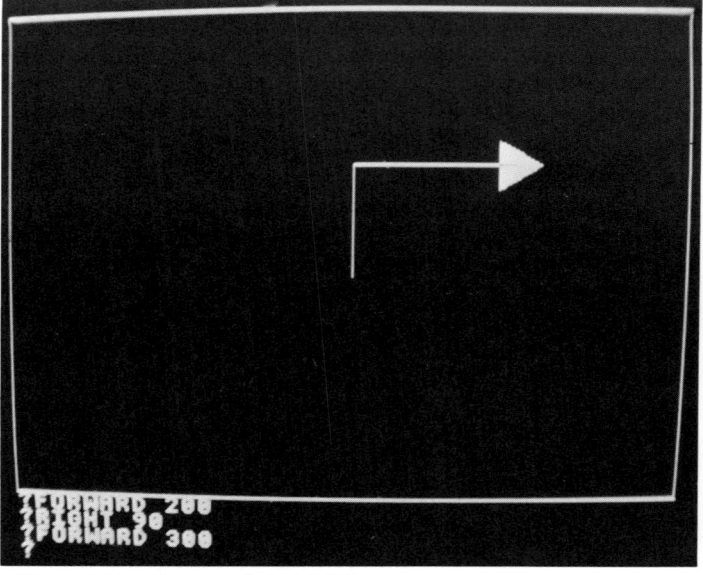

Figure 4.12. Commands in LOGO

What makes LOGO and Turtle Graphics unique, is that it allows the user to define his own keywords. Suppose we are going to produce a display that requires several squares. We can define a word SQUARE by entering:

TO SQUARE

which means I am going to tell the computer how TO draw a SQUARE. The full entry is:

```
TO SQUARE
  REPEAT 4, FORWARD EDGE : RIGHT 90
  END
```

The computer now knows the word SQUARE, so

```
MAKE EDGE = 100
SQUARE
MAKE EDGE = 200
SQUARE
```

will produce the display of Figure 4.13a. Note that the orientation of the square is not fixed. If we clear the screeen and give the instructions:

```
RIGHT 45
MAKE EDGE = 150
SQUARE
```

we would get Figure 4.13b.

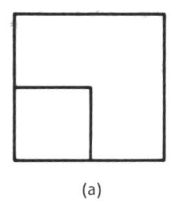

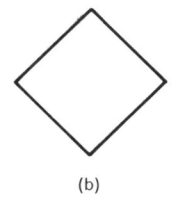

(a) (b) (c)

Figure 4.13. Using defined words in LOGO

Defined words can use other defined words. Suppose we generate a general-purpose word POLY (for polygon) which defines a figure with SIDES defining the number of sides:

```
TO POLY
  REPEAT SIDES, FORWARD EDGE : RIGHT 360/SIDES
  END
```

we can now define:

```
TO SQUARE
  MAKE SIDES = 4
  POLY
END
```

and obviously:

```
TO TRIANGLE
  MAKE SIDES = 3
  POLY
END
```

Before SQUARE or TRIANGLE can be used, the value of EDGE must be entered.

The instructions:

```
MAKE EDGE = 200
TRIANGLE
```

would give Figure 4.13c.

Less obviously:

```
TO CIRCLE
  MAKE SIDES = 20
  POLY
END
```

gives a passable circle.

Surprisingly complex patterns can be obtained from very few instructions. The starfish of Figure 4.14 was given by the following sequence: First we devise a routine to draw a starfish arm (based on half circles)

```
TO ARM
  REPEAT 10, FORWARD DIST : RIGHT 18
  REPEAT 10, FORWARD DIST : LEFT 18
END
```

Next we draw 20 arms spaced at 18-degree intervals:

```
TO STARFISH
  MAKE DIST = 30
  MAKE ANGLE = 0
  REPEAT 20, HOME : RIGHT ANGLE : ARM : MAKE
                                ANGLE = ANGLE + 18
END
```

Figure 4.14. A LOGO starfish

The word HOME puts the turtle back to the middle of the screen pointing up. To get the starfish we enter STARFISH. The word HIDETURTLE, just visible on Figure 4.14, turns the turtle off which was necessary to get a clear photograph.

There are, of course, other features of Turtle Graphics. Defined words can be saved to tape or disk, the MAKE keyword can be used with most of the functions available in BASIC, and the conditional IF is available (e.g. MAKE COLOR = COLOR + 1 : IF COLOR = 5, MAKE COLOR = 1).

In some respects it is unfortunate that LOGO as a complete language has been dominated by Turtle Graphics. LOGO is, in reality, not just a language but a whole educational philosophy of learning by experimentation. Seymour Papert's philosophy of education is described in his thought-provoking book *Mindstorms: Children, Computers and Powerful Ideas*. It should be compulsory reading for all teachers.

FORTH

FORTH is one of the most intriguing languages available for use with microcomputers. Unlike almost every other language, it did not originate in an academic environment, but rather from someone who had a job to do and did not consider any of the available languages to be suitable. The someone was an astronomer, Charles Moore, and the job was controlling one of the telescopes at Kitt Peak in the USA. From this humble beginning, FORTH has grown into a full language (although full is not really the right adjective as we shall shortly see).

FORTH has many unique features, and is totally unlike any other language. The first of these features is the use of a stack to hold numbers. The stack is an area of store that can hold items of data, but these are accessed on a last-in-first-out (LIFO) basis. The best way to visualize this is by thinking of the spring-loaded piles of plates seen in restaurants. As a plate is added, the stack is moved down, and the only plate that can be removed from the stack is the last one to be put in. Sometimes this type of store is called a push-down stack

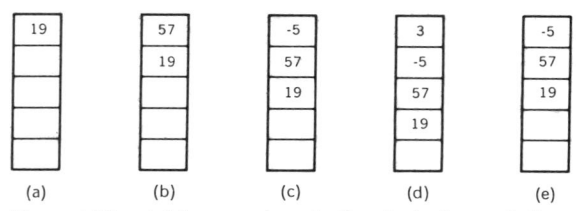

Figure 4.15. Adding numbers to the stack, then printing the top entry

for obvious reasons. To illustrate the procedure, suppose we have an empty stack and we enter 19, 57, −5, 3; the stack will follow the stages of Figure 4.15.

Instructions keywords in FORTH are called just 'words'. The FORTH word equivalent to PRINT in BASIC is a full stop. This removes the top item from the stack and prints it. With the stack as Figure 4.15*d*, this would give a display of 3 and leave the stack as Figure 4.15*e*.

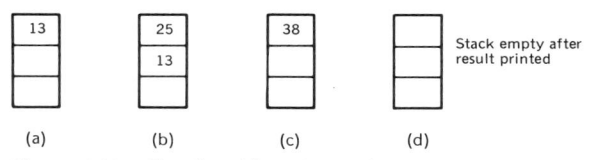

Figure 4.16. Simple arithmetic on the stack

Mathematical operations, +, −, *, /, operate on the top two items on the stack, so 13 25 + . would give the display 38 with the stack visualised on Figure 4.16.

FORTH only works with integers, so the sequence

27 52 + 7 / .

would give the result 11 with the stack operating as Figure 4.17. This is known as Reverse Polish Notation in the jargon,

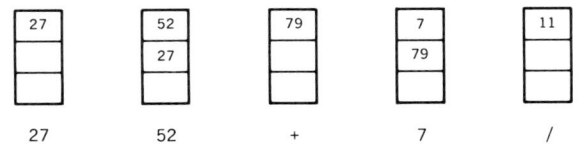

Figure 4.17. More stack arithmetic

and with some ingenuity any mathematical expression can be evaluated. For example:

(12 + 273)*13   becomes 13 12 273 + *
47 − (16*56)   becomes 47 16 56 * −

FORTH includes words to manipulate numbers on the stack. Some of these are:

DROP	Discard the top stack item
DUP	Duplicate the top item
SWAP	Exchange the top two items
ROT	Rotate the top three items so 3rd comes to the top
?DUP	Duplicate the top item if it is non-zero
N PICK	Make a copy, at the top of the stack, of item N (1 PICK is the same as DUP)

There are other stack manipulation words, but the above will serve to illustrate the principles.

Suppose we want to evaluate the quadratic:

$2x^2 + 7x - 3$

for various values of x. Let us suppose x = 5. We start by putting 5 on the stack, then perform the sequence:

DUP DUP 2 * * SWAP 7 * + 3 −

The stack contents, starting with 5 on the stack, are shown in Figure 4.18, through to the result 82 which could, of course, be printed by a full stop. Obviously, the expression could be evaluated for x having other values by starting with a different number on the stack.

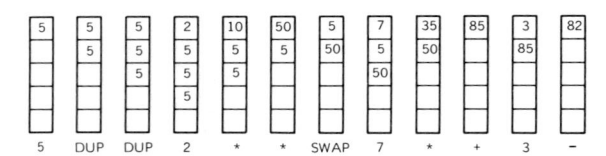

Figure 4.18. Evaluation of the quadratic $2x^2 + 7x - 3$

Messages can be displayed by a full stop followed immediately by quotes space. For example:

." HELLO FOLKS "

would display the message Hello Folks.

The equals sign = has a different meaning in FORTH, in that it tests the top two values on the stack for equality and puts a TRUE (non zero number) or FALSE (zero) on the stack. This can be used by a subsequent IF. . .ELSE. . .THEN as in the example below, which tests if the top value on the stack in 0 (the test could be performed for any number by replacing 0 in the line).

0 = IF ." ZERO " ELSE ." NONZERO " THEN

The first statement is performed if the result of the 0 = is TRUE, the second if FALSE.

FORTH shares with LOGO the unique feature that the user can define his own words. This is done by a colon : followed by the name of the new word that is to be created. The definition of the word follows, being terminated by a semi-colon ;.

To create a word TESTZ, for Test for Zero, we would enter:

```
:TESTZ
  0 = IF
  ." ZERO" ELSE
  ." NON ZERO"
  THEN
  CR;
```

CR is a FORTH word meaning carriage return. ; terminates the definition.

We can now use our word TESTZ

3 TESTZ	gives	NON ZERO
5 3 − TESTZ	gives	NON ZERO
16 8 / 2 − TESTZ	gives	ZERO

The basis of writing FORTH programs consists of creating words which perform small tasks which can be combined until the whole operation to be performed can be defined with one word.

Suppose we want to control some chemical process where we fill a vat with two chemicals, mix them, heat to a certain temperature then empty the vat. We start with a definition BATCH

```
:BATCH
WEIGH1 WEIGH2 MIX HEAT EMPTY;
```

where WEIGH1 etc. are all defined words, for example,

```
:WEIGH1
OPENVI
BEGIN ?TONS1 UNTIL
CLOSEVI ;
```

where OPENVI ?TONS1 CLOSEVI are all defined words.

Similarly:

```
:MIX
MOTORUN
BEGIN ?TIMEUP UNTIL
MOTOROFF ;
```

Each of these words would be defined, probably from other defined words, until definitions can be made in simple FORTH words. At any time, the 'dictionary' can be examined by using the word VLIST.

Obviously this is essentially top-down programming, so FORTH is a good language for writing programs with good style (although it takes some time to adapt to the appearance of the program).

FORTH is a compiled language, which means that the resulting program is very fast (an essential feature in real-time control). In this section we have, of course, only scratched the surface of its capabilities. Mastering FORTH is one of the most worthwhile experiences in computing.

PASCAL

It is difficult to write well-structured programs in languages such as FORTRAN or BASIC. Several languages have developed specifically to encourage the writing of well-ordered programs. ALGOL (for mainframe computers) was one early example from which Professor Niklaus Wirth developed a language called PASCAL (named after the French mathematician and philosopher) with the intention of providing a language which would allow programming to be taught whilst maintaining a logical and systematic style.

PASCAL is thought to be a more difficult language to learn than BASIC (it is compiled, for example, which makes it less friendly). It is true, however, to say that it is easier to learn good programming in PASCAL than in BASIC.

PASCAL includes all the forms of Figure 4.11, and although the evil GOTO is available, its use should hardly ever be necessary. A PASCAL program is essentially written in blocks with the start and finish of blocks defined by the words

BEGIN...END. This makes the form of the program easily visible. For example:

```
IF (some condition)
BEGIN
   |
   (some instructions)
   |
   WHILE (some condition) DO
BEGIN
   |
(some instructions)
   |
END
END
```

One of the problems with illustrating PASCAL is that 'structure' only becomes important on medium to long programs. Any short example therefore looks contrived and even clumsy. The example on the next page is a number guessing game for two players; one enters a number and the other tries to guess it.

This is not a particularly brilliant PASCAL program or game, but is intended to show principles. It is longer than is strictly necessary. It starts with the program title ESP and the fact that it requires both input and output. This is followed by declaration of variables to be used. In our example these are all integers, but PASCAL will also recognise Real, Character and Boolean, and the definition of constants.

Procedure definitions come next. GETNUM gets a number to be guessed from the first player (PASCAL not providing a Random function, this rather contrived method of getting a number was chosen). Note the use of WHILE to check the limits for NUM. The second loop, based on REPEAT...UNTIL, generates 16 line feeds to clear the screen.

The second procedure, GUESSNUM, gets a guess from the second player. Note that "GUESS" is text, and GOES a variable.

The main program starts with a comment (similar to a REM) denoted by the form (*text*). GETNUM, GETGUESS call the

```
PROGRAM ESP(INPUT,OUTPUT);
VAR I,NUM,GUESS,GOES : INTEGER ;
PROCEDURE GETNUM;
  BEGIN
    NUM:=0
    WHILE (NUM > =0)OR(NUM < 100) DO
      BEGIN
        WRITE("GIVE ME A NUMBER");
        READLN(NUM)
      END;
    I:=0;
    REPEAT
      BEGIN
        WRITELN;
        I:=I+1
      END
      UNTIL I=16
  END;
PROCEDURE GUESSNUM;
  BEGIN
    WRITE ("GUESS ",GOES);
    READLN(GUESS)
  END;

(*MAIN PROGRAM STARTS HERE*)

BEGIN
  GOES:=1;
  GETNUM;
  GUESSNUM;
  WHILE GUESS <> NUM DO
    BEGIN
      IF GUESS < NUM
        THEN WRITELN ("TOO LOW")
        ELSE WRITELN ("TOO HIGH");
      GOES:=GOES+1;
      GUESS NUM
    END;
  WRITELN ("GOT IT IN",GOES)
END
```

previously defined procedures, and the WHILE loop requests guesses as long as the GUESS does not equal NUM. Note the use of IF/THEN/ELSE to give limits.

By BASIC standards, the program probably appears complex and a bit odd. (There is := instead of =, for example. PASCAL uses := for manipulation of variables, and = for comparisons. They are not interchangeable.) The important point to grasp, however, is the form of the program, with no confusing GOTOs and a straight logical flow from start to finish.

PASCAL, being a compiled language, requires a large memory, and in almost all cases, disks. (A cassette version of a cut-down Tiny Pascal is, however, available for some machines such as the Tandy TRS 80). Investigating PASCAL consequently involves a fair investment in hardware. It is, however, the most 'professional' of the languages used on microcomputers and as such deserves considerable attention.

COMAL

COMAL, like PASCAL and BASIC, has an educational background. The aim of its Danish designer, Borge Christensen, was to develop a language which combined BASIC's ease of use and friendliness with PASCAL's structure. The resulting language was called COMAL, for COMmon ALgorithmic language.

Superficially COMAL is very similar to PASCAL with minor exceptions. The words BEGIN, END are not used within blocks of programs, for example: but readability is maintained by using the words ENDWHILE, ENDIF.

WHILE condition DO	IF condition THEN	REPEAT
Instructions	Instructions	Instructions
ENDWHILE	ELSE	UNTIL condition
	Instructions	
	ENDIF	

The main advantage of COMAL lies in its user friendliness during program entry and debugging, features which cannot be demonstrated in a book.

As an example of COMAL programming, the example below is a procedure (similar to a subroutine) to move a bat in a video game. The bat can move left (Z), stop (X) or right (C). If no key is pressed, the bat keeps moving in the last direction. The bat position is held in variable X which can vary between 10 (full left) to 35 (full right). Variable D holds +1 for movement to the right, −1 for movement to the left and 0 for stationary.

The procedure could be written in a shorter manner, but has been deliberately written to show the use of the CASE/WHEN/OTHERWISE structure (which is also available in PASCAL).

```
PROC MOVEBAT
   K$ = GET$(0)
   CASE K$ OF
   WHEN "Z"
      X:=X-1
      D:=-1
   WHEN "C"
      X:=X+1
      D:=1
   WHEN "X"
      D:=0
   OTHERWISE
      X:=X+D
   ENDCASE
   IF X:=36 THEN
      X:=35
   ENDIF
   IFX:=9 THEN
      X:=10
   ENDIF
ENDPROC
```

The above procedure would be called by EXEC MOVEBAT.

COMAL is not as freely available as PASCAL or FORTH, but its advantages as a friendly structured language should lead to its wider acceptance in education.

LISP

LISP is a language for manipulating data which is held in lists. Its name is, in fact, an acronym for LISt Processing, (although some people say it stands for Lots of Irritating and Stupid Parentheses). It is actually an old language dating from work done in the early 1960s at MIT. It is, however, eminently suitable for microcomputers and has become the standard language for artificial intelligence research.

In LISP, a list is a set of items enclosed in brackets. For example:

(WHISKY GIN PORT CIDER BEER)

An item in a list can be a 'thing', i.e. a simple item, or another list. A LISP program is, itself, written as a list.

LISP operates by using functions which work on input lists. A typical example is SETQ which is used to assign a list. For example:

(SETQ DRINK'(WHISKY GIN PORT CIDER BEER))

has assigned the list of drinks to DRINK.

Another typical function is CAR which gives the first item in a list. For example:

(CAR DRINK)

would give WHISKY.

LISP allows function definitions with the word DEFUN. For example:

(DEFUN PUT-STOCK (NAME PLACE N1 N2)
   (PUT NAME 'BIN-NO PLACE)
   (PUT NAME 'REORDER N1)
   (PUT NAME 'NOMINAL N2)
   (LIST 'STORES' ENTRY 'FOR NAME))

A typical use of PUT-STOCK could then be:

(PUT-STOCK 'HANDSET 2455 3 6)

Note the way brackets quickly proliferate. An ability to count and keep track of brackets is essential with LISP.

Arithmetic is not LISP's strong point; it is more concerned with manipulating relationships. Normal arithmetic is obtained with the words PLUS, MINUS, DIFFERENCE, TIMES which operate on the words following. For example:

(SETQ X 5)
(SETQ X (PLUS X 3))
(SETQ X (PLUS X 5 22))

will give the result 35 with intermediate steps 5, 8. Similarly,

(SETQ Y(TIMES 16 3))

will give 48.

Division uses the words QUOTIENT and REMAINDER.

LISP, therefore, is a language for manipulating symbols and relationships and as such is a rather specialized language, but one of interest. It is available as an interpreter for most microcomputers.

Other languages

The languages described above are the usual ones chosen as a second language to BASIC. Other languages that may be encountered are briefly described below.

COBOL, one of the original languages, is available for some disk-based micros. Its applications are mainly summed up by its acronym COmmercial and Business-Orientated Language. Since its design (inspired by the US Pentagon in the late 1950s) it has become the standard language for business software.

PROLOG, like LISP, is not a number-crunching language, but is used where symbols, relationships or logical ideas are to be manipulated. (As such it is ideally suited to solving logical problems of the 'John lives next door to the baker, what is the train driver's name' sort of problem.) Like LISP it is widely used in research into artificial intelligence.

Programs written in the language C are compact and fast to run but almost incomprehensible to the uninitiated. For example, $a = i + +$ means make $a = i$ then add one to i, but $a = + + i$ means add one to i then make a equal to the new value of *i*. It is, however, a very well-structured and efficient language. C compilers (and stripped-down Tiny C compilers) are available for some micros but it is not really a language for the beginner.

Other common languages are RPG (RePort Generation), BCPL, ADA (named after Lady Ada Augusta Lovelace, probably the first programmer) which is rigorously controlled by the US Navy to avoid proliferation of dialects and PILOT (a teaching language). It should also be noted that disk-based BASIC compilers are available for some machines.

Machine code

Computers themselves do not understand BASIC, FORTH, PASCAL or any other high-level language. All computers (be they mainframe or micro) only follow instructions written in their own specific code called a machine code. There is not one machine code; each computer or microprocessor has its own. There is therefore a 6502 machine code (which is the microprocessor used by Commodore and BBC machines) and a Z80 machine code (used by Sinclair and Tandy) and a 6809 machine code (used by Dragon) and so on. Unfortunately, different hardware configurations mean that Commodore programs will not run on a BBC, even though the micros, and their machine code, are the same.

High-level language programs are converted to machine code by compilers or interpreters (described earlier) which are machine-code programs written to do the conversion. However, there are occasions (usually when utmost speed of execution is required, or memory size is very limited) when the writing of programs direct in machine code is needed.

Internally a computer can be represented by Figure 4.19. At the machine-code level, the store pigeon holes can only be identified by an address (not a name) and can hold a number in the range 0–255. It is up to the programmer to keep track of what a memory location holds. The number 83 could represent the state of two numbers (8, 3), a binary pattern representing the state of some switches, the straight decimal number, part of a larger number, part of an instruction and so on.

The central processor (CPU) is a microprocessor in most home computers, and contains one of more pigeon holes called registers or accumulators, and an arithmetic unit. Machine-code instructions work with the contents of the registers and store locations.

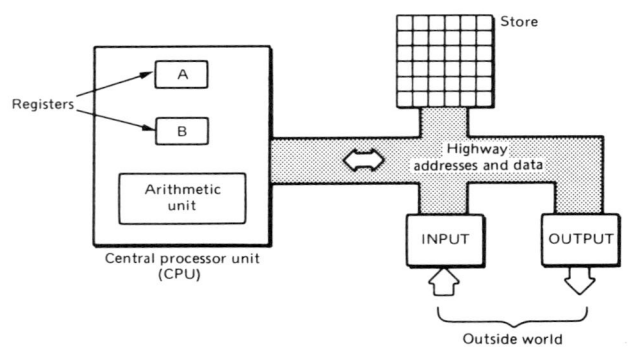

Figure 4.19. A computer as viewed for machine-code programs

There are really very few machine-code instruction types. Almost all are variations on:

FETCH a number from a store location to a register
STORE a number from a register to a store location

(The above two are sometimes known collectively as LOAD)

ADD/SUBTRACT
INPUT
OUTPUT
JUMP to the instruction at a specified store location
Conditional JUMP (IF. . .GOTO)

There are no multiplication or division instructions in most microprocessors.

Machine-code instructions are written in mnemonic form, where one mnemonic represents one, and only one, machine-code instruction. The mnemonics to add two numbers held in location 3220 and 4057, put the result in 6633 then jump to the instruction at 8753 would (loosely based on Z80 code) be:

LD A,(3220)	(first number from 3220 to A)
ADD(4057)	(add second number)
LD(6633),A	(result to 6633)
JP 8753	(jump to 8753)

The mnemonics are converted to the bald binary code by a program called an Assembler (similar in operation to a compiler).

Programming in machine code requires intimate knowledge of both the language of the microprocessor used, and the actual hardware of the machine itself. It is not particularly difficult, but requires more care and thought (a fault in a machine-code program will probably cause a total crash and the loss of the program. Control will only be regained by turning the machine off and on again). It is, however, the most rewarding experience in computing. Machine-code programming, with examples, is discussed in more detail in *Beginner's Guide to Microprocessors*.

5

Disks, files and records

*All things are taken from us, and become
Portions and parcels of the dreadful Past.*

Tennyson

Introduction

All programs need data, and in general this can be entered into the program in three ways:

1. As part of the program using DATA statements which are READ
2. By the user in the course of the running of the program via prompts and INPUT statements.
3. From large back-up storage systems.

Method 1 is really only suitable for data that changes infrequently because the program needs to be amended to change the data. Method 2 is the most useful for a program where data does not need to be carried forward from one execution of the program to the next, because all data is lost when the computer is turned off.

Let us suppose that we were organizing a computer record system for an estate agent. This would need to store houses for sale and allow the user to query the system for '3-bedroom semi-detached bungalow in the Milton area in the range £30 000 to £40 000'. Obviously this is an ideal job for a computer, but one in which the details of probably several hundred houses would need to be stored. These details will change daily as houses are sold or new ones offered for sale.

Method 1 is obviously totally out of the question, as the system would not be very cost-effective if the services of a computer programmer were needed every evening.

Method 2 might work, but all the house details would have to be re-entered every time the computer was turned off. Whilst it is possible to leave a machine on for 24 hours a day, supply interruptions from the electricity boards are surprisingly common. Switching of feeds and transformers by the boards can cause loss of supply for a few tenths of a second; not long enough to notice but enough to corrupt a computer's memory (one good reason for saving incomplete programs every 30 minutes or so when typing in a long program). It is therefore somewhat risky to hold the details in the computer memory.

Method 3 would use some form of magnetic storage, disk or tape. These hold their contents permanently and are not affected by the absence of power (they can even be sent through the post). The only really effective way to hold our house records is to use backup storage which can be interrogated, and amended by the computer.

There is another factor to consider, however, and that is the amount of storage. To make our house records meaningful, we would need to store at least the following:

Owner's name	30 alpha
House address	40 alphanumeric
Owner's address	60 alphanumeric
Day phone	12 alphanumeric
Evening phone	12 alphanumeric
House type	3 numeric
Number of rooms	2 numeric
Area	3 numeric
Asking price	6 numeric
Date on market	6 numeric
Enquiries	3 numeric
Comments	40 alphanumeric

The numbers are a rough estimate of how many characters each item may need. A few items may need some explanation. The house address and owner's address may differ, but as the house address is local the full postal address is not needed. The owner's address will, however, need full postal address, and hence is longer. House type is a 3-digit code arranged as Figure 5.1, and the area code is similar. Enquiries are the number of people shown round the house, and Comments is available for any special features.

Each character takes up one store location, so one house record requires 217 store locations. 200 records require 43 400 store locations, which would leave little, if any, room for a program in most small computers.

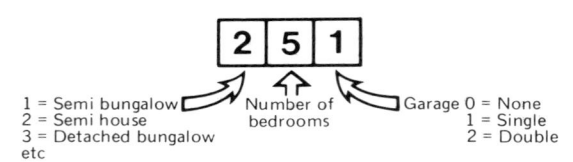

```
          ┌───┬───┬───┐
          │ 2 │ 5 │ 1 │
          └───┴───┴───┘
```

1 = Semi bungalow   Number of   Garage 0 = None
2 = Semi house   bedrooms   1 = Single
3 = Detached bungalow   2 = Double
etc

Figure 5.1. Possible coding for house type. This can obviously be extended to include more details

It could be argued that all records will not be 217 characters long. This is true, but a computer system that works only on average lengths of records rather than maximum will one day run into trouble. In addition, as we shall see shortly, it is easier to deal with files if each item in the file is arranged to be a fixed length.

There are, therefore, two reasons for using magnetic tapes or disks as backup storage where records or files are needed:

(a) The stored data does not vanish when the machine is turned off (it is 'non-volatile' in the jargon).
(b) In most applications requiring files, the required storage capacity is beyond that available in the computer's store.

Items, fields, records and files

So far we have used the terms items, records and files rather loosely. To explain them in a bit more detail, consider how an estate agent would organize his house particulars with a card system. Each house would have a card arranged along the lines of Figure 5.2b. Each of these cards, which holds all the particulars of one house, is a 'record'. The record consists of several descriptive 'items', one of which is shown on Figure 5.2a. Often the word 'field' is used in place of item. A collection of records as Figure 5.2c, is called a 'file'. Items of fields make records make files.

A file can be defined as a set of related records which are organized in some way. Related is important, because there is little point in making a file where one record holds details of a house for sale, and next one details of a customer's mortgage. Organized is also important, because there must be some way that a particular record can be located, and the items used.

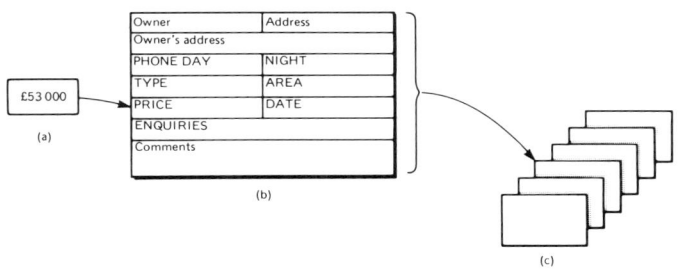

Figure 5.2. (a) An item, (b) a record and (c) a file

There are a few jargon words associated with files. Reading data from a file is called 'accessing' the file. Adding a new record or modifying an existing record is called 'updating'. Searching through a file for a specific combination of field data (e.g. 6-room detached houses in Minster) is called 'interrogating'. Often, an organized set of files is called a 'database'.

Types of file

There are basically two types of file: serial and random. These terms refer to the way in which the file is accessed. In a serial file, all the records are arranged serially one after each other. A file recorded on a tape recorder is inherently serial. To get a specific record, the machine must work its way through all preceding records. The time taken to get to a record depends on where the tape currently is and the location of the required record.

A random access file allows the user to go direct to a required record. For practical purposes, disk-based files can be random access, because the read/write head can be moved to any track quickly, and the time taken for the required sector to come round is, by human standards, very short.

It does not follow, though, that all disk files are random access and all tape files are serial access. It is possible (and sometimes advantageous) to use serial files on disks, and given computer control of the fast forward/rewind/play on a tape recorder, it is possible to have passable random-access files on tape. The mini-cassette of Figure 2.19 has such features.

There are several subdivisions of serial files. A sequential file has the records arranged in some order (e.g. alphabetical ordering of names, or numerical ordering by age for example). An indexed file is preceded by an index which gives 'keys' into the file following. It could, for example, hold all the surnames of people in a file with the surname followed by the record number. This speeds up the access to a given record.

We shall return to serial and random access disk files shortly.

Cassette files

If the constraints of a cassette are recognized, it is possible to use cassette-based files quite effectively. With a domestic cassette player, the computer can only start/stop the tape.

Cassette files are useful in two circumstances. The first, and commonest, is to store some data whilst the computer is powered down (or as security against computer failure). The amount of data to be stored must be such that it can *all* be held in the computer. The sequence is usually:

1. The computer is powered up and the program is loaded
2. The cassette data is loaded
3. Required operations are performed
4. New data saved to cassette
5. Machine turned off

It is usual, but not necessary, to arrange the cassette data to be stored in the computer in some form of array. The sailboard race outlined earlier used cassette files to store entrants' details and results from day to day.

Cassette files are also useful where data is to be written serially to a file to build up some form of history. Logging data (probably automatically) from a long-running experiment is one example, recording stock movement out of a works stores is another. In each case, data is written serially onto the tape for subsequent analysis.

Cassette files cannot be used interactively. It is not possible to modify one record on a cassette file on its own. To achieve this effect the whole file must be loaded into the computer, the changed record amended in the computer, and a brand new file created. This is rather tedious, and it follows that a cassette file cannot be larger than the computer store using it (although this restriction can be overcome with some ingenuity). It would not be feasible, for example, to use cassette files for an estate agent's program.

Two examples of cassette files are given below. Both are based on the BBC computer which has one of the better systems for handling cassette files.

The first example is a very simple telephone directory which consists of two separate programs. The first creates the directory and the second loads it from cassette and interrogates it. In practice, of course, a useful program would combine both and provide options for modifying/adding details, but such a program would be unreasonably long for inclusion in this book. The reader may like to consider how such a program could be developed from the example below.

```
100 DIM S$(10), F$(10),P$(10)
110 PRINT "THIS PROGRAM CREATES A FILE OF 10 PHONE
    NUMBERS"
120 FOR I=1 TO 10
130 PRINT
140 PRINT "RECORD";I
150 INPUT "SURNAME";S$(I)
160 INPUT "INITIALS";F$(I)
170 INPUT "PHONE NO";P$(I)
180 NEXT I
190 REM NOW SAVE TO TAPE
200 X = OPENOUT ("PHONE")
210 FOR I = 1 TO 10
220 PRINT #X,S$(I),F$(I),P$(I)
230 NEXT I
240 CLOSE #X
250 PRINT "FILE SAVED"
```

Lines 100 to 180 dimension the arrays and input the data from the keyboard, the actual file creation takes place at lines 190–240. Communication to and from a file takes place via an intervening 'buffer store', which assembles blocks of data for recording on the tape. The instruction OPENOUT allocates a buffer to the named file "PHONE". The buffers are numbered, and line 200 puts the buffer number chosen by the computer into variable X. OPENOUT also displays the message 'Press Record then Return' on the screen to tell the user to start the tape recorder.

The actual data is recorded by the loop around line 220. PRINT #X means 'Send the following data to the file accessed by buffer X'. Data is assembled into blocks in the buffer and sent to the tape. CLOSE #X says we have finished with the file, and causes any incomplete block currently in the buffer to be sent to the tape followed by an end of file marker. This marker (usually called EOF) tells any program reading the file that the file is complete and no further data is to be read.

A program to interrogate the file is very similar:

```
100 DIM S$(10),F$(10),P$(10)
110 X = OPENIN("PHONE")
```

```
120 I = 1
130 REPEAT
140 INPUT #X,S$(I),F$(I),P$(I)
150 I = I+1
160 UNTIL EOF #X
170 CLOSE #X
180 INPUT "ENTER SURNAME";Q$
190 MARK = 0
200 FOR I = 1 TO 10
210 IF S$(I)=Q$ THEN PRINT P$(I):MARK=1
220 NEXT I
230 IF MARK = 0 THEN PRINT "NOT FOUND"
240 GOTO 180
```

The file is read at lines 110 to 160. OPENIN allocates a buffer to the file "PHONES" and puts the buffer number in X. INPUT #X reads data from the tape and puts it into the named variables.

It is essential that the PRINT statement and INPUT statement match. Data is written onto the tape with no identifier as to what it is. If we wrote to the tape with

PRINT #X A$,X,B,Z$

and read back with

INPUT #X X,A$,Z$,B

the program would fail because the string in A$ would be read back into numeric variable X with disastrous results. Data *must* be read off the tape in the order it went on. If it goes on Name, Initials, Age, Address, that's the order it will come off.

A REPEAT/UNTIL loop is used to read the data from the tape into the directory arrays. EOF is used as the terminator of the loop. The CLOSE instruction stops the tape and clears the input buffer. The arrays loaded from the tape can then be interrogated via lines 180–240.

A serial cassette file cannot be edited on the cassette. To add, or modify, entries we would need to INPUT# the old file, modify the arrays as required and PRINT# the new file. If more records were being added it would be necessary, of course, to modify the DIM statements.

The above programs have many shortcomings. They cannot, as they stand, deal with duplicate surnames. The reader might like to consider how they can be improved.

The second example below shows how a data logger program can write experimental data to a cassette file at regular intervals. This uses two features of the BBC computer. TIME is a variable on the BBC which increments at 0.01 second intervals, and ADVAL(1) is an input that converts a voltage measurement to a digital number. This would be the parameter being measured in the experiment. The program records ADVAL at 1-minute intervals for 4 hours.

```
100 TIME = 0 : OT = 0
110 X = OPENOUT("LOG")
120 REPEAT
130 D = ADVAL(1)
140 PRINT #X,TIME,D
150 REPEAT:UNTIL TIME-OT >=6000
160 OT = TIME
170 UNTIL TIME > 1440000
180 CLOSE #X
```

The operation of this program is straightforward. Line 150 determines the time interval at which samples are taken (every minute) and line 170 the total time over which the experiment runs (4 hours). For this program to work, the computer must have control of the recorder's play control. This is normally provided on domestic cassette players via a 2.5 mm jack socket adjacent to the microphone input socket.

Disk-based files

The placing of records onto a disk (and the subsequent recovery) is quite a complex operation. A disk is divided into tracks and sectors, and the correct track/sector must be selected to write/read a record. Fortunately all this complexity is made totally transparent to the user by a disk-operating system (DOS).

A DOS is a program which handles all the complexity of data transfer to and from the disk, and lets the user use disk-based records without worrying where on the disk a record is actually placed. There are many types of DOS; CP/M is one of the more professional, but there is no common standard. The examples below are based on Tandy TRSDOS which is, in the author's opinion, one of the more straightforward operating systems.

File names

A single disk can hold many files and programs. These must all have unique names so they can be individually identified. Typical file specifications are:

    YACHTS/DAT.EAP:1
    PERT/BAS:0
    WAGES/AUG:1
    ACCIDENT/TXT.RCJ:0
    PAYROLL/FTN.SESAME:1
    GAMES:0

The first part is the file name: YACHTS, PERT, WAGES etc. The second part (which must always be three letters and be preceded by /) is called the extension, and is used to further identify the file. It can be used to identify what the file contains (DAT, data file; BAS, BASIC program: TXT, text; FTN, Fortran program) or as a further description (as in AUG for August). The extension is not mandatory (as in GAMES) and can be any three letters.

The third part, preceded by a full stop, is a Password (EAP, RCJ, SESAME). This is optional, but if used must always be given in subsequent Read/Writes to gain access to the file. Passwords do not appear on any listings of disk contents, and are intended to give added security to files. If a password is used, care should be taken to remember it; a file cannot be used without it and there is no way of finding out what the password is.

The final part (:1, :0) indicates which disk drive the file is to be used on. The drive number is preceded by a colon.

Serial-access files

TRSDOS provides for both serial- and random-access files. Serial-access files are used in an almost identical manner to the cassette files outlined earlier, apart from some minor dialect differences and a vast increase in speed. We will amend the cassette telephone directory program for disk use.

A serial disk file is accessed via an intermediate buffer in an identical way to that outlined for the cassette file. IN TRSDOS the user specifies the buffer number, so line 200 of the telephone file creation program becomes:

200 OPEN"O",1,"PHONES/DAT.EAP:0"

"O" means open the specified file for output, 1 is the buffer number, and "PHONES/DAT.EAP:0" is the file name.

If the file does not exist, a file is created with the specified name. If the file name exists, all data on that file is lost, and a new file is created with the specified name.

Writing to the file is almost identical. The only difference is the buffer number is specified directly. Line 220 becomes:

220 PRINT #1, S$(I),F$(I),P$(I)

The CLOSE statement (which writes EOF to the disk) does not require the # symbol, so line 240 becomes

240 CLOSE 1

With these minor exceptions, the disk program to save the phone directory to the disk is identical to the cassette program.

Reading the file is also similar, but it is important to remember that, like the cassette, data is read strictly in the order that it was written. OPENing the file for input puts a 'marker' pointing to the first item on the named file, and subsequent inputs take items of the file in order with the marker keeping track of which record is next to be read. The program portion below corresponds to lines 110 to 170 of the cassette file reading program. Line 100 and 180 onwards are unaffected.

```
110 OPEN "I",1,"PHONES/DAT.EAP:0"
120 K = 0
130 IF EOF(1) THEN GOTO 170
140 INPUT #1,S$(K),F$(K),P$(K)
150 K = K+1
160 GOTO 130
170 CLOSE 1
```

As an aside, TRS BASIC does not have REPEAT/UNTIL, which causes a less elegant program with two evil GOTOs.

Serial disk files suffer from the same disadvantage as cassette files. Because OPEN "O" clears any existing file of the same name it is not possible to *directly* modify or add to a serial file on the disk. The file must first be loaded, in total, into the computer (probably into arrays), the modifications made and the new file written back to the disk.

It is, however, possible (if somewhat tedious) to use and modify serial-access files which exceed the memory capacity of the computer. There is no problem writing data to the file; data can be input from the keyboard to the file to the limit of the capacity of the disk. To read data, the file must be opened and read in until the required record is reached. For example, the program portion below reads, and displays, a specified record. OPEN "I" puts the position marker to the start of the file, then all records up to, and including, the required one are read into the same variables. When the FOR/NEXT loop finishes, the variables contain the required data.

```
100 INPUT "RECORD NUMBER";N
110 OPEN "I",1,"CLASS/DAT:1"
120 FOR J = 1 TO N
130 INPUT #1,NAME$,AGE$
140 NEXT J
150 PRINT NAME$,AGE$: REM ON TV SCREEN
```

This method does not need store-gobbling arrays.

Modifying large serial files requires a temporary dummy file with a different name. The procedure is best described as a procedure list:

(a) Open source file for input
(b) Open dummy file for output
(c) Read small blocks of source file into memory, modify or add data, and write to dummy file
(d) Repeat (c) until all of source file has been modified and transferred to the dummy file
(e) Close both files
(f) Delete source file
(g) Rename dummy file to name of original source file.

Serial disk files are therefore simple to use, but rather difficult to modify. Like cassette files they are best suited to holding relatively small amounts of data whilst the computer is turned off.

Random-access files

A file user requires to be able to go to any record and read or modify it directly. This is difficult to achieve with serial-access files. Random-access files allow the user to go directly to a record, although they do require some care in their use and place some constraints on the user.

The most important of these constraints is the fixed-length record. A record in a random-access file is always the same length; 255 characters in TRSDOS. Within each record, the length of each individual item is defined by the user, but fixed thereafter. Unused character positions in item 'fields' are padded out with spaces as shown on Figure 5.3a. Compare this with the serial file of Figure 5.3b.

The first decision that a user of a fixed-length record has to make is the allocation of the 255 characters. Figure 5.4 shows the probable allocation of characters for records in the estate agent's house file described at the beginning of this chapter. This allocation is done via the FIELD keyword, as we shall see shortly.

Reading and writing of data is, again, done via a buffer. With random-access files the buffer will only hold one 255 character record at one time. The keyword FIELD allocates

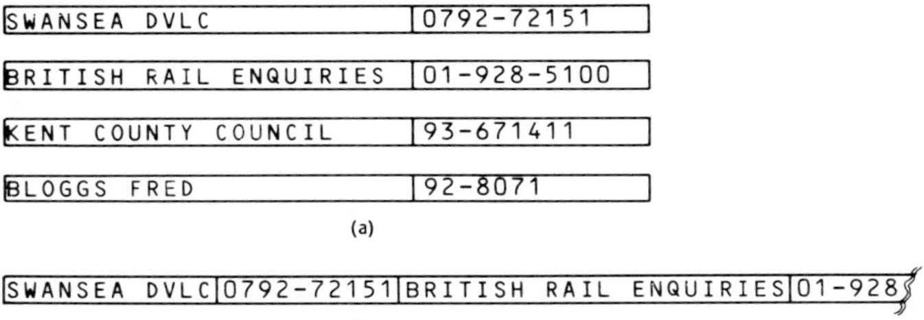

SWANSEA DVLC	0792-72151
BRITISH RAIL ENQUIRIES	01-928-5100
KENT COUNTY COUNCIL	93-671411
BLOGGS FRED	92-8071

(a)

| SWANSEA DVLC | 0792-72151 | BRITISH RAIL ENQUIRIES | 01-928... |

(b)

Figure 5.3. Comparison of (a) fixed-length record and (b) serially arranged file

character positions in this buffer to string variable names. The record in Figure 5.4 would be set up by:

FIELD 1,30 AS OW$, 40 AS AD$, 60 AS OA$, 12 AS DP$,
        12 AS EP$, 4 AS HT$, 3 AS NR$, 4 AS AR$,
        7 AS AP$, 7 AS DT$, 4 AS EQ$, 40 AS CM$

This rather long instruction says how to set up buffer 1 (the buffer number comes immediately after FIELD). The rest of the instruction details the number of characters in the buffer (and hence the file record) to be allocated to each string

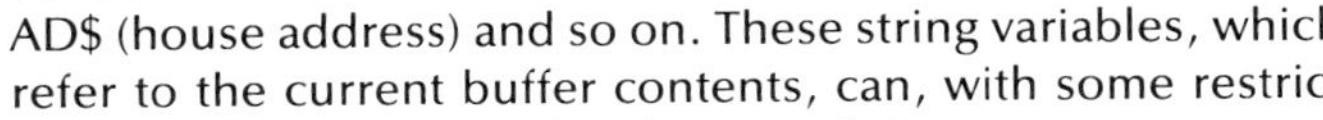

30	40	60	12	12	4	3	4	7	7	4	40
OW$	AD$	OA$	DP$	EP$	HT$	NR$	AR$	AP$	DT$	EQ$	CM$

Figure 5.4. A random-access file record

variable. The first 30 are OW$ (owner's name), the next 40 are AD$ (house address) and so on. These string variables, which refer to the current buffer contents, can, with some restrictions, be used normally by the rest of the program.

Let us now see how we use a random-access file with house details. First we open the file:

    OPEN "R",1,"HOUSES/DAT.ZAP:1"

Where R denotes buffer 1 is random access. A buffer set up for random access can handle input and output (unlike serial files where the direction has to be specified).

Next the buffer is set up using FIELD as described above.

Data is loaded from the computer to the buffer by the word LSET. This operates similar to LET, except the buffer variable is padded out with spaces to the correct length. If, for example, we have:

```
100 INPUT "Owner's Name";Q$
110 LSET OW$ = Q$
```

and we enter Smith John A (which takes up 12 characters); OW$ will be padded out with 18 spaces so it occupies the full 30 character field. Each item in the buffer is entered in a similar manner. When the buffer is complete, the instruction PUT is used to write the buffer contents to the disk. This takes the form:

PUT buffer, record

so PUT 1,12 will put the contents of buffer 1 into record 12 in the currently open file.

To read from the disk, GET is used. This has the same format as PUT, so GET 1, 147 will bring the contents of record 147 to buffer 1, where it can be examined via the allocated variable names.

As an example, let us assume we want to change the asking price for a house. This can be done via the program segment below, which assumes that the file is already OPEN and the buffer FIELD has been done. TR is the top record number:

```
500 INPUT "HOUSE ADDRESS";Q$:L = LEN(Q$)
510 I = 1
520 GET 1,I
530 IF LEFT$(AD$,L) = Q$ THEN GOTO 550
540 I = I + 1 : IF I > TR PRINT "NOT FOUND" :STOP
545 GOTO 520
550 PRINT "CURRENT PRICE";AS$
560 INPUT "NEW PRICE";NP$
570 LSET AP$ = NP$
580 PUT 1,I
590 CLOSE 1
```

Lines 500 to 545 search for the house in the file by getting each record in turn and looking for a match with the input address. Because AD$ is padded out with spaces, the match must be checked to the length of Q$, hence the need for LEFT$. When a match is found the buffer contains all the details of the required house.

Line 550 prints the current price, using the buffer variable AP$. Line 570 changes the value (leaving the rest of the buffer unaltered) and the amended buffer is written back to the disk at line 580.

The above is not a very forgiving program. It would not, for example, match '30 Albert Street' to '30 Albert St', but it shows the principle.

Random-access techniques

The use of random-access files has several advantages. In particular:

(a) Any file can be read directly without having to start at the first record
(b) Reading and writing can take place through the same buffer
(c) It is easy to modify one item in a record (unlike serial files where the entire file has to be read, modified and rewritten)
(d) The file can be much larger than the computer memory

To obtain the full benefit of random-access files, however, requires careful planning. In particular the program will need some form of 'key' to get the right record number from some input data (e.g. the home address above). In our simple example we did a search record by record for a match. This is adequate for small files, but can be slow for large files.

One common solution is to load a cross-referencing array at the start of a file accessing program. The match search can then be done in the computer memory which will only take a fraction of a second. In our house details program, for example, we could set up an array consisting of the first 12 letters of each house address (which should be unique). The file record number for a given address can then be found quickly from the computer's memory.

Random-access files deal only with characters. When numbers are to be stored, these must be first converted to strings. This can be done with the function CHR$ or the TRSDOS functions MKD$,MKI$ or MKS$ which are similar. When reading data from the disk, VAL$ (or the TRSDOS CVD, CVI, CVS) converts a string back to a number.

Operating system utilities

A disk operating system provides many useful routines for manipulating files and programs on disks. Some of the more common are given below (using TRSDOS terminology).

DIR (for directory) lists all files on a disk. DIR:1 could give

FILE DIRECTORY – DRIVE 1   TRSDOS   12/03/84

ACCID/BAS P
HOUSES/DAT
PHONE/DAT
YACHT/DAT   ESTATE/BAS
RACE/BAS P   PHONES/BAS

The suffix P denotes password-protected files.

FORMAT is used to put the sector/track markers on new blank disks. This must be done before the disk can be used.

COPY makes a duplicate file (and allows the file name to be changed if desired).

BACKUP copies an entire disk to another disk to give protection against accidental loss or damage. Any serious user of files should perform regular backups of all important disks.

KILL deletes a named file.

FREE displays the spare space on a disk.

Most operating systems have far more utilities, but the above are those more commonly used.

6

Games, graphics and sound

Chess problems are the hymn tunes of mathematics.
                                                    G. H. Hardy

Introduction

Probably 75 per cent of home computers are used solely for playing games. This is not really surprising as the graphics and sound capabilities of even the cheapest modern machines are at least as good as a dedicated games console. In addition, the cost of a games cassette is under one third of the price of the ROM based cartridges needed on a games console.

This preponderance of games playing is viewed with some disdain by some people, who consider that computers should be used for 'serious' purposes. In practice, games playing is an excellent introduction to computing; it is fun, it bring out all the best in the capabilities of the machine and takes away the fear of the machine that many people have. Attempting to modify, or write, games is an excellent way of learning about computers. A lot of experience can be gained (in both programming ideas and debugging) from entering a games program from a magazine and getting it to work.

This chapter discusses games techniques as a basis for understanding graphics and sound features. First, however, we must briefly see how a TV picture is produced by a computer. The description below is rather simplified; for more details the reader is referred to the companion book *Beginner's Guide to Television*.

Television pictures

Most people know that a television is constructed of lines; 625 in the British standard, 525 in the USA. These lines are 'drawn' by a tiny beam of electrons which produce a 'spot' on the TV screen. The spot is moved over the screen to produce

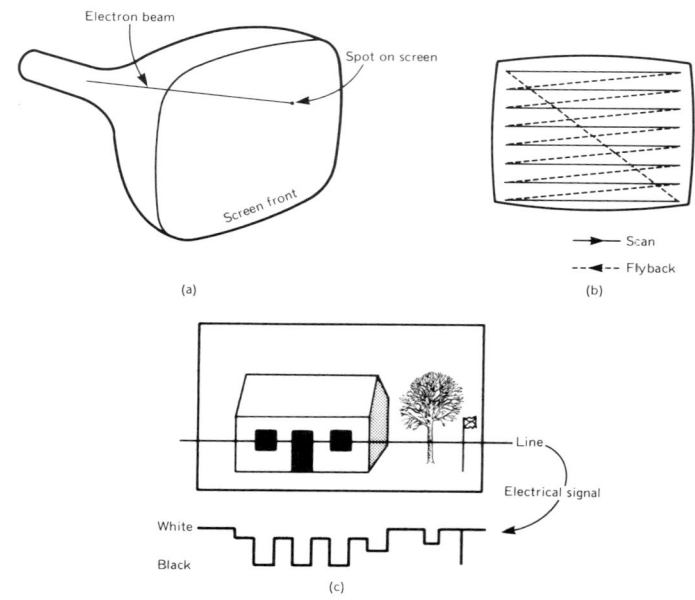

Figure 6.1. Production of a TV picture. (a) TV tube; (b) TV lines formed by scanning (8 lines shown; TV picture uses 625); (c) TV picture and one line

the familiar line pattern of Figure 6.1b. The spot moves very fast, covering the whole screen in 1/50th of a second, so its movement is too fast to follow.

As the spot moves, its intensity is varied by an electrical signal representing the required picture. Figure 6.1c shows the electrical signal for one line of a television picture. Because the spot movement across the screen is too fast for the eye to follow we see the whole screen illuminated with a picture.

Producing a TV picture therefore requires electronics to move the spot (which is provided by the television itself) and an electrical signal representing the light/dark areas of the picture (which normally comes from the TV station, but we will supply from the computer).

Displaying text

The simplest form of display involves only text, so we will deal with this first. Let us assume the display shown in Figure 6.2 which is 40 characters wide and 25 rows high (the standard used on Teletext). This is known as a 40 column by 25 row display. One computer store location can hold a

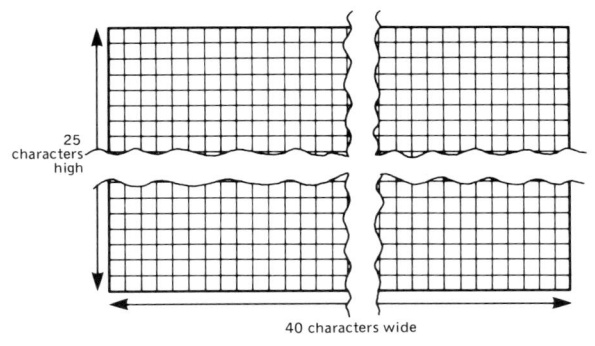

Figure 6.2. Standard 40 × 25 character display

number in the range 0–255 which, if taken as an ASCII character (see Chapter 2), will hold all the alphanumeric characters we will need. Notable exceptions are the ZX81 and Dragon, which do not hold their video data in ASCII, but in their own code.

A simple schematic of a common arrangement is shown in Figure 6.3. To display 40 × 25 characters requires 1000 store locations. An area of store with addresses, say, from 4000 to

4999 is used to hold the characters to be displayed on the screen. This is known as the Video RAM, and its size and address range varies from machine to machine.

The video RAM is also read by a circuit called a character generator. This goes through the characters held in the store, and produces the necessary light/dark electrical signal for the television. How it does this need not concern us. Character generator circuits are discussed in the author's companion book *Beginner's Guide to Microprocessors*.

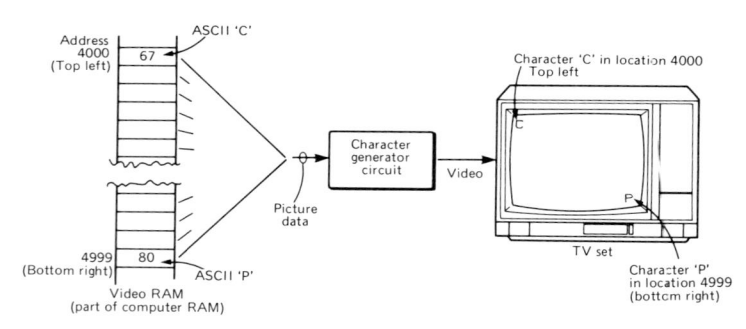

Figure 6.3. Producing characters from the video RAM to the television screen

If we assume that address 4000 corresponds to the top left of the screen, and 4999 to the bottom right as in Figure 6.3, we can work out the address for any screen position from the simple formula:

Address = 40*(R−1) + (C−1) + 4000

where R is the row number (1 to 25) and C is the column number (1 to 40). If, as is more usual, the rows are numbered 0 to 24 and the columns 0 to 39, the address is given by:

Address = 40*R + C + 4000

Let us suppose we want to put a letter M into column 14 on row 10. First we need to know the ASCII code for M. Table 2.1 gives us 77.

Next we need the address; putting C = 14 and R = 10 gives

Address = 40 × 10 + 14 + 4000 = 4414

We therefore need to put 77 into address 4414 and an M will appear on the screen.

There are two common ways of achieving this from a BASIC program. The first uses PRINTTAB(C,R) which prints subsequent text at column C row R. To print the letter M at column 14 row 10 we would use:

PRINTTAB(14,10);"M"

It should be noted there are dialect variations between machines. Some use PRINT @ C,R, some SCREEN(X,Y) and some PRINT@N where N is calculated in a way similar to the address calculations above. The Spectrum uses PRINT AT but puts *row* first *column* second.

The second, and faster way, uses the BASIC word POKE. This allows a value to be entered directly to a store location. It usually takes the form

POKE Address,Value

so POKE 4414,77 would display an M at column 14 row 10.

POKE is a slightly dangerous function and its use should be tempered with care. It is not possible to damage the machine itself, but it is very easy to wreck a BASIC program by POKEing into an incorrect address. Always make a tape or disk copy before running a program containing POKE instructions.

BASIC also has a function called PEEK which returns the value of a store location. Let us suppose we want to find out what is displayed at column 17 row 5. The address is 4217 (calculated as above) so we write:

Q = PEEK(4217)

The variable Q now contains the ASCII value of the character at column 17 and row 5. If, for example, the position contains *, Q would have the value 42 which is the ASCII code for *.

It is possible to obtain the address/value for PEEKs and POKEs from variables, as the simple program below shows:

```
100 INPUT "GIVE ME A COLUMN";C
110 INPUT "AND A ROW";R
120 INPUT "AND AN ASCII VALUE";N
130 AD = 40*R+C+4000
140 POKE AD,N
```

It must be emphasized that there is almost no standardization between different machines. Each has a different number of rows and columns, each its own range of video RAM addresses. There is not even agreement as to whether Column 0 Row 0 is top left or bottom left of the screen. These essential facts will, however, be given in the machine's handbook.

Introduction to graphics

There are basically three types of graphics used on home computers. These are commonly known as block graphics, pixel graphics and line graphics.

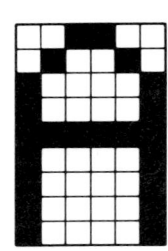

Figure 6.4. One character position based on a 6 × 9 dot matrix

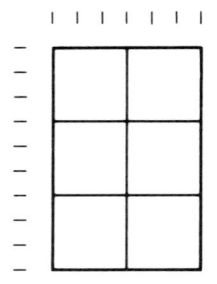

Figure 6.5. A 6 × 9 character cell split into 6 pixels

Each character on a computer display is built up from dots similar to Figure 6.4. There are, inevitably, variations but a typical machine would use 6 by 9 dots per character. It follows that a 40 × 25 character display has a potential resolution of 240 dots horizontally and 225 dots vertically.

Block graphics only allow the user to change individual character positions. This is not quite the restriction it might seem. ASCII coding uses numbers 0 to 127 to represent alphanumeric characters. A store location can hold a number in the range of 0 to 255. Block graphics assign values 128 to 255 to graphic symbols.

Pixel graphics breaks each character position down into 2 × 3 squares as Figure 6.5. Each square is called a pixel. With 40 × 25 character positions, pixel graphics has a resolution of 80 × 75 pixels.

Line graphics allows the programmer to address each individual dot on the screen. This gives access to the full resolution of the machine. A typical high-resolution line graphics machine will use a resolution of 640 × 256 dots which is at the limit of most domestic televisions. As we shall see shortly, this resolution is achieved at the expense of additional storage.

Block graphics

Although the user of a machine with block graphics is limited to the character rows and columns, surprisingly good results can be obtained by ingenious use of the graphic symbols. These include a range of lines, blocks and gaming symbols such as men, cars, playing card symbols and so on. Some of these are shown on Figure 6.6.

Using block graphics is very similar to writing text at a given column and row. The required graphics code is either POKEd direct into the video RAM or written with PRINTTAB(C,R)CHR$$) where C is the column position, R the row and N the graphics code. If a given symbol is to be used many times, a more readable program is obtained if a string variable is assigned to the graphics code. Suppose, for example, the graphics code for a man symbol is 237. Early in the program we can write

   LET MAN$ = CHR$(237)

thereafter we use MAN$ whenever we want a man. For example:

   PRINTTAB(5,14)MAN$

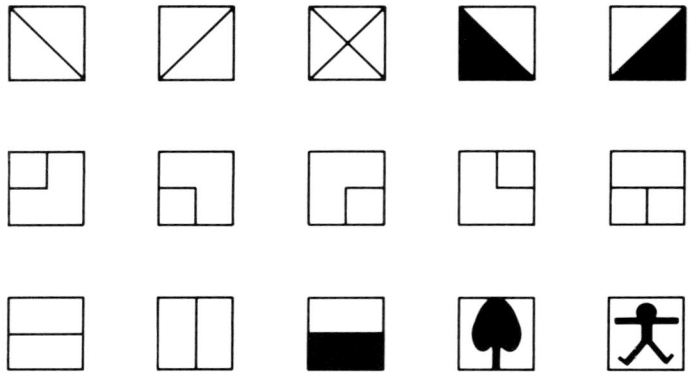

Figure 6.6. A selection of block graphics symbols (most machines have many graphics symbols)

Loops can be used to advantage. Suppose we want to draw a line of men from columns 10 to 25 on row 3. Assuming MAN$ has been assigned as above, this can be achieved with:

```
1000 FOR C = 10 TO 25
1010 PRINTTAB(C,3)MAN$
1020 NEXT C
```

User-defined characters

Many machines (notably the VIC-20, Commodore 64 and BBC) allow the user to define graphic characters in the program. There are many variations on how this is achieved, but the method used on the BBC will show the principles.

A user-defined character is based on an 8 × 8 grid of dots as Figure 6.7a. Numbering from the right, the columns are numbered in powers of 2, i.e. 1, 2, 4, 8 etc., up to 128 on the extreme left. The required symbol is now drawn on the grid as shown for the man of Figure 6.7b. The value of the dots in each row is then evaluated as shown.

The instruction to assign this character to a graphics code number (say 241) is:

VDU 23, 241, 28, 28, 8, 127, 8, 20, 34, 65

VDU 23 is the keyword saying we are about to define a graphics character and 241 is the graphics code number. The remaining 8 numbers are read direct off Figure 6.7b. The definition only needs to be done once in a program; thereafter CHR$(241) or POKEing 241 into the video RAM would produce a man.

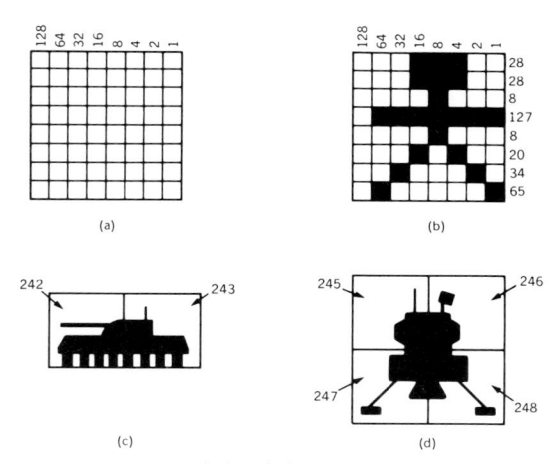

Figure 6.7. User-defined characters. (a) user-defined grid; (b) a man symbol; (c) a tank from 2 characters; (d) a lunar lander from 4 characters

Graphics symbols can be produced using more than one character position. Figure 6.7c shows the two halves of a tank. If these were assigned graphics codes 242 and 243 as above, a tank variable, TK$, could be formed by:

LET TK$ = CHR$(242) + CHR$(243)

PRINTing TK$ anywhere on the screen will now give a tank symbol occupying two character positions.

By using linefeed (LF) and backspace (BS) composite characters can be built up in both horizontal and vertical directions. The lunar lander of Figure 6.7d, for example, would be obtained by:

LL$ = CHR$(245) + CHR$(246) + LF + BS + BS + CHR$(247) + CHR$(248)

Sprites

The design of games such as space invaders are made much easier by the use of user-definable characters, but these can only be drawn in one colour. Some machines (notably the TI 99/4A and the Commodore 64) allow movable multicoloured user-defined characters which are known prosaically as MOBs (for movable object blocks) but more poetically as Sprites.

Sprites can be moved as a block themselves, and some machines allow a depth definition which allow sprites to pass in front of, or behind, other sprites on the screen for full dimensional effects. Sprite collisions (e.g. laser bolt hits spaceship) are easy to detect, which simplifies many games.

Moving characters

Suppose we have drawn a man at column C and row R on the screen with C = 0 and R = 0 being top left. The relationship of adjacent screen positions is shown on Figure 6.8a; to move up we would take one off R; to move diagonally down and left we would take one off C and add one to R.

Figure 6.8b shows the same movements in terms of video RAM where A is the address of the current position (calculated as explained earlier) and NC is the number of columns on the screen. To move left one character position we subtract one from A. To move diagonally up and to the right we subtract NC and add one.

Figure 6.8 tells how to move characters around the screen. First we decide the direction we want to move the character from some form of player input; probably the keyboard or a joystick. Knowing the direction we want to move, we can work out what change is needed to the column and row positions (or to the video RAM address if POKE is being used). The old character is erased by writing a space to the

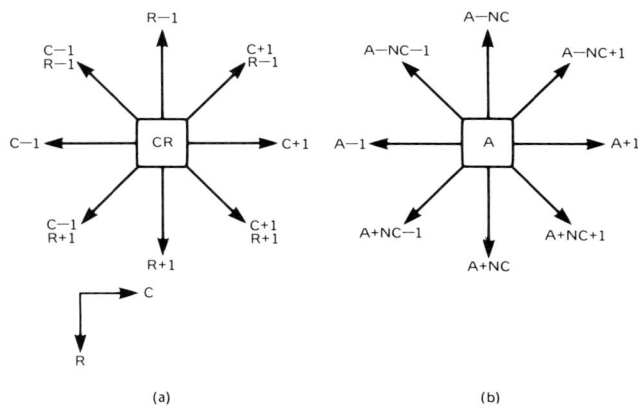

Figure 6.8. Movement about the screen: (a) in terms of rows and columns; (b) in terms of video RAM address

old character position. The character can then be written to the new column and row position. By moving the character at regular time intervals a very realistic animation can be obtained.

Detecting collisions

Many games need to detect collisions; balls hitting bats, bullets or laser bolts hitting spaceships and so on. A collision is easily detected by PEEKing at the video RAM address that a character is about to move to. If it contains a space (ASCII code 32) the position is clear. If it contains any other character a collision is about to take place and suitable action can be taken.

A typical example is shown in Figure 6.9 which represents a ball travelling round a squash court. The ball is moved by changing C by an amount DC and R by DR. Initially on track (a), both DC and DR are −1. At point A the ball collides with

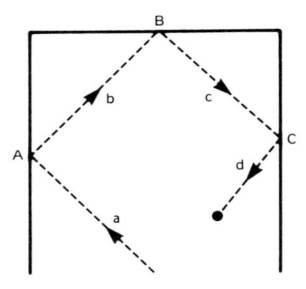

Figure 6.9. Moving a ball around a squash court

the wall. DC changes to +1 giving DC = +1, DR = −1. At point B another collision changes DR to +1. Finally at point C, DC changes to −1 leaving DC = −1, DR = +1 for track (d).

Pixel graphics

A machine with pixel graphics is often said to have medium-resolution graphics. The user can control individual square pixels; typically 80 horizontally and 75 vertically although there are considerable variations between machines.

A single text character position can typically be divided into two horizontal and three vertical pixels as shown earlier in Figure 6.5. It follows that there is an easily calculated relationship between character and pixel positions, but inevitably this relationship will vary from machine to machine.

Pixels are controlled by three BASIC keywords. The first two are concerned with turning pixels on and off:

SET(X,Y)

turns ON the pixel at horizontal position X and vertical position Y, and

RESET(X,Y)

turns OFF the pixel at horizontal position X and vertical position Y.

These two simple instructions allow surprisingly intricate pictures to be constructed, such as the spaceship of Figure 6.10.

The third instruction, POINT(X,Y) gives the value of 1 if the pixel at the point X,Y is ON, and 0 if the pixel is off. This is used to examine the state of a pixel to test for a collision or some such event. For example:

1000 X = X+DX : Y = Y+DY
1010 IF POINT(X,Y) = 1 THEN GOSUB 3000

where the subroutine at line 3000 could be an explosion.

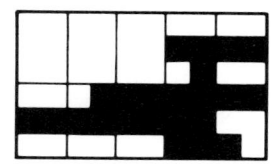

Figure 6.10. A spaceship with pixel graphics

Figure 6.11. Filling a solid area

Loops can be used to fill solid areas. The square in Figure 6.11 has corners at X1, Y1 to X2, Y2. This can be drawn by the inner and outer loops below:

500 FOR J = X1 TO X2
510 FOR K = Y1 to Y2
520 SET(J,K)
530 NEXT K
540 NEXT J

Diagonal lines, such as Figure 6.12, can also be drawn with a loop but this is slightly more complicated. To get a continuous line it is first necessary to find out which is the larger:

(Y2 − Y1), (X2 − X1). The larger direction, X or Y, is then used as the loop counter. Simple arithmetic then gives the value of the other direction from the loop counter. For example, suppose X2 − X1 is the larger:

```
800 FOR X = X1 TO X2
810 S=(Y2 − Y1)/(X2 − X1) : REM LINE SLOPE
820 Y=INT( (X − X1)*S) + Y1
830 SET (X,Y)
840 NEXT X
```

Line 810 calculates the slope of the line, actually the tangent for the mathematically minded.

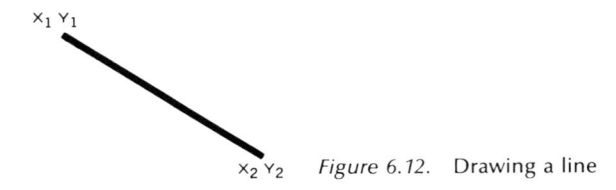

Figure 6.12. Drawing a line

Many machines with pixel graphics also incorporate block graphics, which allows the programmer to combine two techniques to maximum effect.

Line graphics

High-resolution graphics allow the programmer to control individual dots on the screen. The BBC, for example, in its highest-resolution mode uses 640 × 256 dots and the Spectrum 256 × 176. This is at the limit of resolution of the average television, but is obtained at some expense.

Block and pixel graphics use one store location per character position, and need about 1000 store locations. The character generator circuit determines which dots on the screen need illuminating. A line graphics machine stores the full dot pattern in its store. The BBC, for example, needs to store 640 × 256 dots. Each store location can hold the state of 8 dots, so simple arithmetic shows that 20 480 store locations

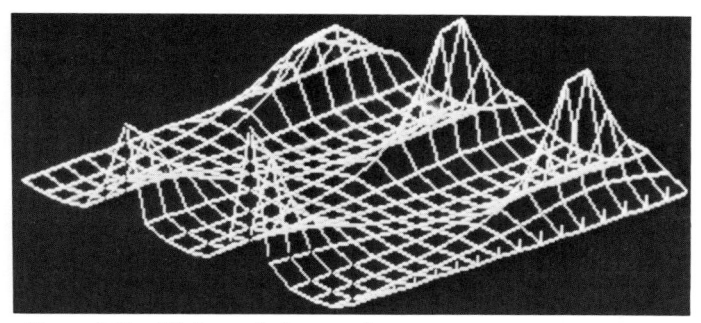

Figure 6.13. High-resolution graphics

are needed for the video RAM. A microprocessor can use 65 000 store locations. The BASIC interpreter itself will use about 16 000 locations, so high-resolution graphics severely reduces the store space left for the program itself. The results are very impressive though, as Figure 6.13 shows.

The 0,0 origin of text and block graphics screens is usually at the top left-hand corner of the screen. Rather confusingly, the 0,0 origin of a line graphics is usually at the bottom left-hand corner and is numbered as shown on Figure 6.14.

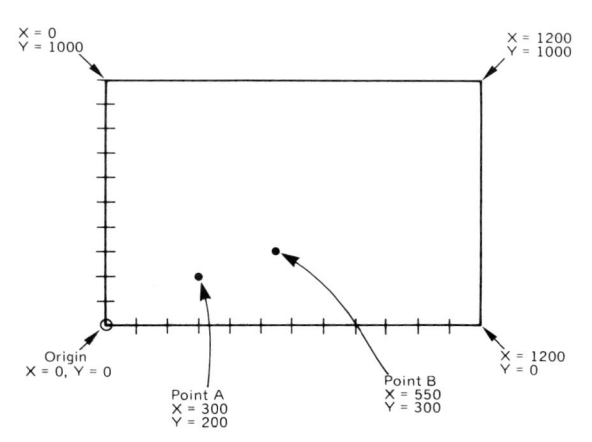

Figure 6.14. Points on a high-resolution display

175

The X,Y range of numbers is actually greater than the resolution, but this is of little concern to the user. Point A is at X = 300, Y = 200, B at X = 550, Y = 300 and so on.

There are three commands used with line graphics, but it should be noted that there are considerable differences in terminology between different machines. The principles are the same, however, and all use the idea of a 'graphics head'. The head is similar to the idea of the LOGO turtle described earlier in Chapter 5.

The first command, which we shall call MOVE (X,Y), moves the head to position X,Y without leaving any mark on the screen.

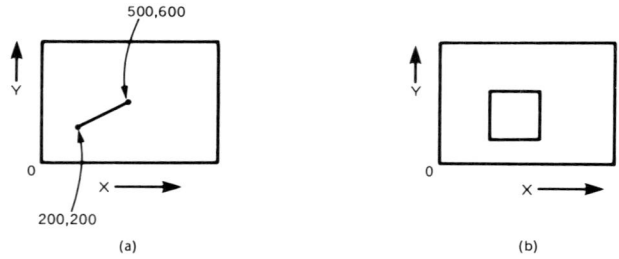

Figure 6.15. The DRAW instruction: (a) drawing a line, (b) drawing a square

The second command, which we shall call DRAW (X,Y), moves the head to position X,Y, but leaves a line drawn on the screen from the last head position. If we are at X = 200, Y = 200 and obey the instruction DRAW (500,600) we would get Figure 6.15a. The instructions to draw the square of Figure 6.15b are therefore:

```
100 MOVE (200 200)
110 DRAW (600 200)
120 DRAW (600 600)
130 DRAW (200 600)
140 DRAW (200 200)
```

The first MOVE instruction moves the head to the bottom corner of the square without leaving a trace. A common error amongst beginners is using a DRAW for the first point of a figure. This leaves a line across the screen from the last head position.

Solid areas can be filled either by using loops to fill the area with adjacent lines (as demonstrated earlier for the solid square drawn with pixel graphics) or by a FILL command (a FILL command is not available on some machines, notably the Spectrum). There are two ways a FILL command works: one based on a triangle and one on a rectangle.

The triangle method, used on the BBC, fills the area bounded by the current position and the last TWO points visited by the head. Figure 6.16a would be filled by the instructions:

```
100 MOVE(100,100)
110 MOVE (300,200)
120 FILL (600,100)
```

(As an aside, the BBC does not use the word FILL, but the much less descriptive PLOT 85. More explicit are keywords such as the Dragon PAINT.)

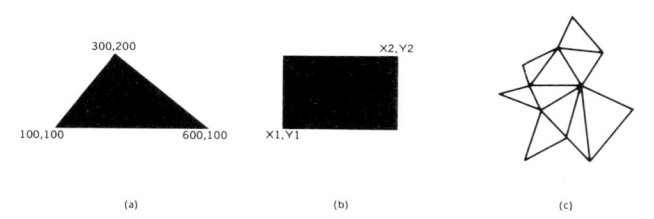

Figure 6.16. The FILL instruction: (a) FILL with a triangle, (b) FILL with a rectangle, (c) a complex shape filled with triangles

The rectangle fill method (used by the Dragon and others) defines a rectangle with opposite vertices X1,Y1 and X2,Y2 (given with the FILL keyword) as shown on Figure 6.16b. The rectangle is then filled. Both methods have their advantages and disadvantages, although it is easier to fill complex shapes such as Figure 6.16c with triangles.

Often POINT (X,Y) is provided. This returns a number representing the colour of the specified screen position. For example:

1500 C = POINT(X,Y)
1510 IF C=3 THEN PRINT "LANDED"

We shall return to a discussion of colour later.

There are many additional line graphics instructions: CIRCLE (for drawing whole and part circles), DOT (for illuminating a single point or dotting lines) and so on. These functions, and their availability, vary tremendously from machine to machine so the reader is advised to study his User Manual with care.

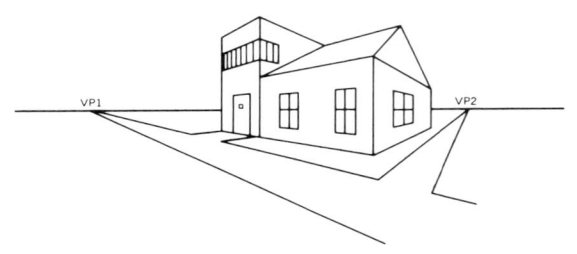

Figure 6.17. A perspective line drawing

A certain knowledge of elementary geometry and trigonometry is desirable to use line graphics to best advantage. Without this knowledge, the drawing of perspective drawings such as Figure 6.17 is a bit difficult. One alternative is to sketch out what is required on squared paper then build up a table of points which can be entered into the program in DATA statements which are READ to draw the required picture.

Vector graphics

There is a fourth type of graphics which is not currently available on any home computer, but is widely used on industrial computer-aided design machines, some arcade and one home games console (Vectrex). This uses the computer output to directly move the electron beam spot and draw the image on the TV screen (as opposed to the normal method where the computer controls the intensity of a scanned spot). This method is known as vector graphics, and gives very high resolution. Unfortunately it needs a special monitor so it is unlikely to be used on home computers in the near future.

Colour

Close examination of a colour television picture will show that it is composed of tiny red, green and blue spots. Almost any colour can be constructed by suitable combinations of red, green and blue. For simplicity, computers driving colour TVs only turn spots on or off. If we denote ON by 1 and OFF by 0 we get:

R	G	B	*Colour displayed*
0	0	0	Black
0	0	1	Blue
0	1	0	Green
0	1	1	Cyan
1	0	0	Red
1	0	1	Magenta
1	1	0	Yellow
1	1	1	White

Some of these may seem odd, yellow in particular, but these are additive colour mixing. Paint colours are obtained by subtractive colour mixing.

The programmer has the choice of eight colours for the background and the graphics/text. These are usually called the background and foreground colours, but the foreground and background colour for text can be changed almost letter by letter on computers which are Teletext-compatible.

Colour changes take computer store space which is, as we have already seen, reduced by line graphics. On the BBC computer, for example, there is a trade-off between resolution and the number of colours available.

Mode	Resolution	Colours	Memory usage
0	640 × 256	2 (Black/White)	20 K
1	320 × 256	4	20 K
2	160 × 256	8 + Flash	20 K
3	TEXT ONLY	–	16 K
4	320 × 256	2 (Black/White)	10 K
5	160 × 256	4	10 K
6	TEXT ONLY	–	8 K
7	Teletext	8 + Flash	1 K

Teletext mode is essentially block graphics and uses control characters to change colour. It is very economical on memory space.

The current colour for foreground and background is changed by BASIC keywords. These vary, inevitably, from machine to machine, but probably the most descriptive are those used by the Sinclair Spectrum:

INK N sets the current foreground colour to N
PAPER N sets the current background to N

where N is a number defining the colour (e.g. N = 1 means red, 2, green, and so on). Selecting a new INK colour does not affect any previously drawn lines; only subsequent lines are drawn in the new colour. PAPER overrides previous PAPER instructions.

Animation with coloured line graphics is done in essentially the same way that was described earlier for block graphics; the object is erased then redrawn in the new position. What may not be obvious is that a coloured object is erased by redrawing it in the same position with the INK colour same as the PAPER colour.

Player inputs

The player can control a game either from the computer keyboard or from joysticks. The latter is to be preferred as the keyboard will take quite a battering from a game such as Defender.

Two common BASIC keywords are used to obtain keypresses from the keyboard (INPUT is obviously of little use as the Enter button has to be pressed to continue the program).

GET$ *waits* for a single key to be pressed, then gives the corresponding single character string. The Return key is not used. For example:

```
200 PRINT "DO YOU WANT INSTRUCTIONS Y OR N"
210 Q$ = GET$
200 IF Q$ = "Y" THEN GOTO 5000
230 IF Q$ = "N" THEN GOTO 1000
240 GOTO 210
```

GET$ is useful for selecting options from a menu, but is not suitable for controlling a fast-moving arcade game. For that we need the next keyword.

INKEY$ scans the keyboard to see if a key has been pressed (and returns a single character string if a key has been pressed). Unlike GET$, though, INKEY$ does not wait for a key. If no key is pressed, INKEY$ returns an empty string. For example:

```
500 D$ = INKEY$
510 IF D$ = "X" THEN XD = +1
520 IF D$ = "Z" THEN XD = −1
530 IF D$ = "." THEN PROCFIRE
```

There are two forms of joystick control. The first, and simplest, consists of four switch inputs to the computer, one, or possibly two, of which are made at any time to show the position the joystick handle has been moved. This requires a digital (On/Off) interface into the computer and can resolve eight directions (45 degrees). A more sophisticated joystick uses potentiometers to give a very fine measurement of the handle position. With care, a resolution of better than 1 degree in any direction can be obtained.

Whichever type of joystick is used, it is possible that some form of interface circuit will need to be purchased. Many home computers are supplied with the circuits necessary to scan a joystick. Although these interface circuits are quite simple, would-be home constructors are warned that connection of home brews will probably invalidate the warranty.

Using the joystick in a program is very simple. There is no standard BASIC keyword, but as an example, the BBC uses ADVAL(N) where N is a number specifying which (of four) inputs is to be read. Four inputs allow for two players, each with a two axis joystick. ADVAL returns a number in the range 0 to 64 000 dependent on the joystick angle. A typical program segment could be:

```
600 J1 = ADVAL(1)
610 IF J1 >= 45000 THEN XD = +1
620 IF J1 <= 15000 THEN XD = -1
```

Fire buttons are invariably a digital input, and are read as an ON/OFF signal.

Types of games

There are really three types of games available for computers, which we can loosely classify as Cerebral, Arcade and Adventur. Cerebral games are games of logic against the computer.

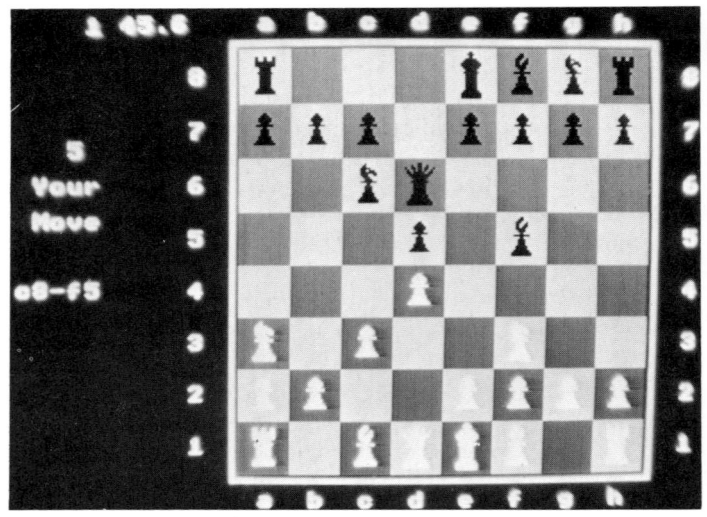

Figure 6.18. Playing chess against a computer

The most common are chess (see Figure 6.18) and backgammon. It used to be said, just a few years ago, that a computer would never play a good game of chess. However, the programs now available will easily beat the average player and will even give the better player a hard game. The author has never beaten the program of Figure 6.18, and it is a salutory experience to be outclassed by a computer!

Figure 6.19. An arcade game with high-resolution graphics and sound

The second type of game, the arcade, is illustrated by 'Killer Gorilla' on Figure 6.19. These test a player's reaction time and reflexes, have excellent graphics and are fast and noisy. It is difficult to obtain the necessary speed with BASIC (see Chapter 4 for ways of speeding up BASIC programs) so most commercial arcade games are written in machine code.

Adventure games are unique, being based on the role playing game 'Dungeons and Dragons'. The computer contains the details of an underground complex of caves or the layout of a rambling mansion. The player explores this 'world', searching for treasure whilst battling with monsters and solving logical problems. These are not games to be played in one go; to explore fully the simplest will take days or weeks; the author took two years to traverse the original 'Adventure' game on a DEC 11/34 computer. The extract below is from the 11/34 game 'Dungeon'.

```
>KILL TROLL WITH SWORD
The fatal blow strikes the troll square in the heart: he dies.
Almost as soon as the troll breathes his last, a cloud of
sinister black smoke envelops him, and when the fog lifts, the
carcass has disappeared.
Your sword is no longer glowing.
>E
You are in a north-south crawlway; a passage also goes to the east.
There is a hole above, but it provides no opportunities for climbing.
>S
You are in what appears to have been an artist's studio. The walls
and floors are splattered with paints of 69 different colors.
Strangely enough, nothing of value is hanging here. At the north and
northwest of the room are open doors (also covered with paint). An
extremely dark and narrow chimney leads up from a fireplace. Although
you might be able to get up the chimney, it seems unlikely that you
could get back down.
```

Incidentally, the author would be pleased to learn what use can be made of the inflatable rubber boat in 'Dungeon'.

The essential part of playing (or writing) an Adventure game is to draw a map as you go along. Figure 6.20 shows part of the map for the original 'Adventure' game. Most objects have a use (e.g. the wand produces a bridge across the chasm), some have side-effects.

A good adventure has a maze:

'You are in a maze of twisty little passages, all alike'.

Sometimes the junctions are identified by subtle changes of text:

'You are in a twisty maze of little passages, all alike'.

Another solution to mazes is to turn unidentifiable junctions to identifiable junctions by leaving objects, e.g.

'You are in a maze of twisty little passages, all alike.

There is a gold bar here'.

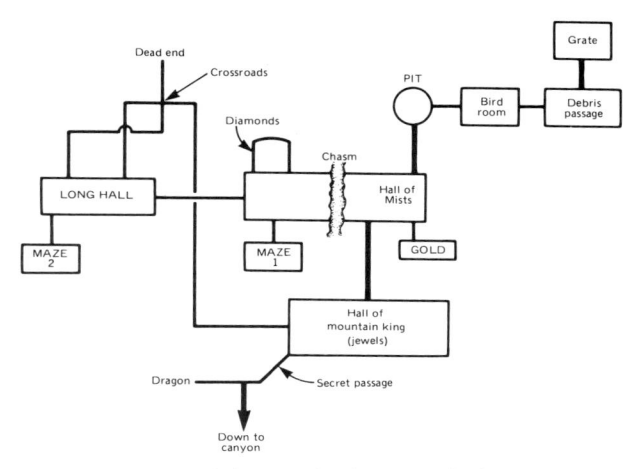

Figure 6.20. Part of the map for the original adventure game. This represents less than 10 per cent of the game and has been simplified to avoid giving hints to other players!

Adventure games are unique in that they take the form of narrative text, and rely little on sound or graphic effects. It is rather like reading a book, except that you are the hero, and the plot is different every time you play.

Sound effects

Sound is one of the least standardized aspects of home computers, and varies from the rather feeble 'Beep' of the Spectrum to the almost synthesizer sound of the BBC or Commodore 64.

In general, a given sound has three characteristics: its pitch, its harmonics and its envelope. Noise, a special sort of sound, does not have the first two but we will return to this topic shortly.

The pitch of a note, whether it is high or low, is determined by its frequency. Middle C on the piano, for example, has a frequency of 261 cycles per second. The higher the frequency, the higher the note sound.

A sound wave is actually pressure variations in the air. A pure note, which sounds rather boring, has a pressure wave similar to Figure 6.21a (called a sine wave for the technically-minded). Real-life sounds, such as a piano, have more interesting shapes such as Figure 6.21b which make the note sound 'richer'.

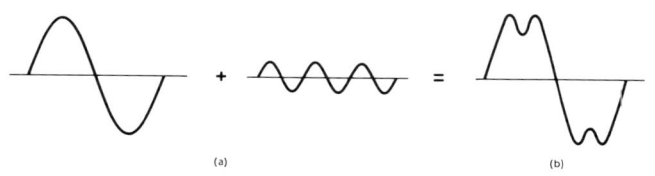

Figure 6.21. Sound harmonics. (a) The component sine waves. (b) The resulting shape.

It can be shown that any waveform can be formed by adding pure notes together. The lowest note is called the fundamental (and determines the pitch we hear). The others are called the harmonics, and it can be shown that they are some integral multiple (2, 3, 4 etc.) of the fundamental.

Any real-life note does not turn on and off instantly. The sound can come up quickly and turn off slowly, as Figure

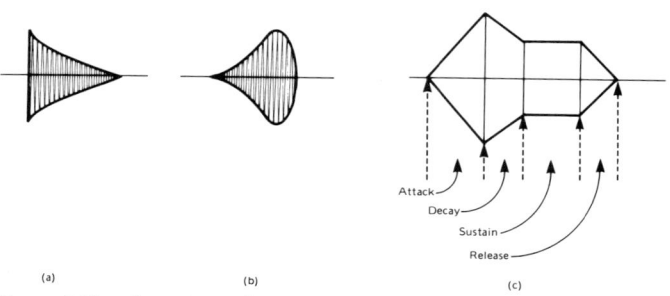

Figure 6.22. Sound envelopes. (a) Fast attack, slow release. (b) Slow attack, fast release. (c) Envelope definitions

186

6.22a, or start slowly and finish quickly, as Figure 6.22b. This shape is called the envelope, and is generally represented by the envelope of Figure 6.22c which has four identifiable sections called Attack, Decay, Sustain, Release. The amplitude and duration of these should be individually controllable.

Noise is sound which does not have a pitch as such. Steam hiss from a steam engine, thunder, a gun shot, and interference on a radio are all noise. Most games require noise for gunfire, spaceship engines, explosions and so on. The envelope of a noise is very important; it is the envelope that distinguishes a machine gun sound from the chuff of a steam train.

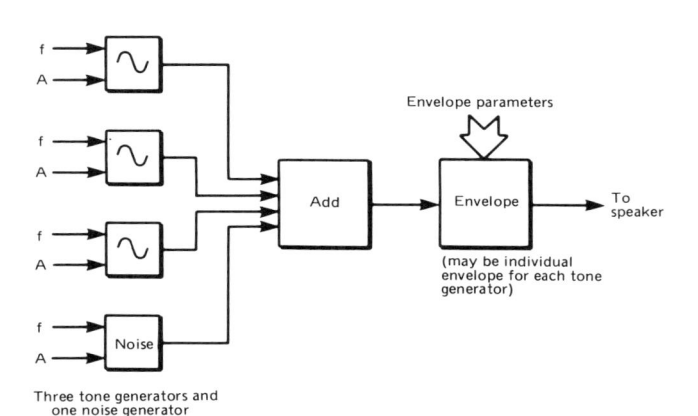

Figure 6.23. A typical sound generator

Even if we cannot identify the pitch of noise, one can talk about high-frequency noise (steam hiss) and low-frequency noise (explosions with bits coming down, thunder). Some form of 'frequency' control is therefore needed with noise.

With the above requirements, we end up with a sound generator similar to Figure 6.23. Three pure-tone generators are provided to give three notes or one harmonically rich note. Each has its own frequency and amplitude (volume) control. The noise generator has an amplitude control and a coarse frequency control. These are all added and fed to the envelope circuit. The envelope parameters and all the frequency/amplitude controls are set by keywords from BASIC.

As may be gathered, producing a sound is rather complex if all the features are used. It is very entertaining, though, to write a small program that allows experimentation with the various sound parameters.

7

Computer applications

Somehow it seems to fill my head with ideas – only I don't know exactly what they are!

Lewis Carroll

Introduction

Classically, computing has been divided into three areas, namely scientific, commercial and control. Scientific computing uses the mathematical computational power of the computer for applications such as the production of astronomical and nautical tables, engineering calculations for, say, stress analysis in bridges, statistical analysis of experimental results and so on. These are all essentially programs which are run once to produce a definite result, and probably require little by the way of mass storage.

Commercial computing is found in banks, businesses, government departments and insurance companies. The calculations are largely trivial, but are done on vast amounts of data. Large-mass storage is required to hold, say, people's bank accounts. The programs are also repetitive, being run on a regular (daily/weekly/monthly) basis.

The use of computers for industrial control is one of the more intriguing applications. Computers are used to control oil refineries, steel mills and nuclear power stations. The use of colour monitors (called VDUs for Visual Display Units) for plant mimics gives operators a clear indication of the state of the process under control. The requirements for a control computer are high speed (because the real world will not wait) and large input/output capability to handle all the plant sensors and actuators.

Classically these divisions have lead to the development of three different types of computer. To some extent the microcomputer has tended to blur these distinctions, and has lead to the idea of a general-purpose computer. Although no one would seriously suggest that you could run a nuclear power station with a Spectrum or manage the DVLC at Swansea with a Dragon, the microcomputer is a 'Jack of all trades' that will do many jobs very well.

This chapter examines some applications of microcomputers, and technical developments which will increase the effect of them on our lives in the future.

Education

Governments are not noted for being forward-looking, but praise is due to all parties for the Microelectronics Education Programme (MEP) first announced by a Labour Government in 1978 but implemented by the Conservatives after the 1979 election. Originally conceived as a £9 million four-year project, the aim was to provide computing facilities in all secondary schools by subsidizing half the cost of approved British microcomputers. In practice, the majority of machines purchased have been Research Machines 380Z and 480Z, BBC and Sinclair Spectrums. The scheme has since been extended in time, finance and scope to cover peripherals (and items such as Turtles), primary schools and special educational needs (such as deaf children).

The effect of this has been dramatic. It raised the awareness of teachers and pupils, and solved the old problem of schools buying different, and hence incompatible, machines. It has consequently become possible to establish a stock of educational programs and a core of expertise which can be shared amongst schools on a county basis.

There have, of course, been difficulties. Initially, in most schools the teachers and children started learning together; with the children leading most of the time! Teacher training has been a rather hit-and-miss affair, and has largely been based on short 'awareness' courses rather than longer courses on the use of computers for education. As a result there has been a certain amount of agonizing in schools along the lines of 'We've got it, we know how to connect it all together and get it working roughly, but what do we DO with it?' Inevitably, some schools have gone off at tangents. It is fair to say that the gains obtained in computer education are directly proportional to the interest and efforts of a schools staff.

The easiest area to define is 'Computer Studies' or 'Computer Awareness'. This commends itself to teachers as it is a solid subject that is eminently teachable and progress can be measured by tests and examination. It is, nonetheless, a

Figure 7.1. A typical 'select the answer' program: a geography test

worthwhile topic as computers will undoubtably impinge on everyone's life in the future. The limitation in most schools is the lack of computers. It is not possible to learn programming by rote learning; time at a keyboard is essential. Pupils with two computers between a class of 35 will have little time at a keyboard.

Computers can also be used to teach other subjects, but again a lack of machines is a problem. There is considerable discussion about the form this should take. The simplest programs, of which the geography test of Figure 7.1 is typical, work on the old principle of 'select the correct answer from the list'. More sophisticated programs use the excellent graphic facilities of modern computers to demonstrate principles in, say, physics, and simulate experiments.

At the primary-school level, computers are used with success to aid literacy and numeracy. The programs are often based on the children's game of 'Hangman', or present the child with problems to be solved on an adventure-type treasure hunt.

One interesting, and unexpected, use of computers is the development of a child's social skills. Many programs lend themselves to group work; Yellow River Kingdom, where

Figure 7.2. Even playing arcade games can be education. The machine is the BBC model B, widely used in schools

children run a small city, is one of the simpler. Business simulation programs are an example of more advanced group work. Many teachers have been surprised how a group, working together to make decisions, often reveals a child's talents and can help to bring a shy child out of his shell. Even playing arcade games in a lunchtime computer club (Figure 7.2) can be beneficial.

The requirements for educational software are stringent. The programs must be interesting and of just the right intellectual level; not too difficult, but not too patronizing. Instructions must be clear and concise, and clearly show whether ENTER is required at the end of an entry or a single key press. The best way to achieve this is by consistency throughout the program, but if this is not possible colour-coding of prompting text is a useful way of showing what is expected.

Above all, programs must not crash regardless of what a child does. This means the Escape and Break keys must be

Figure 7.3. The BBC buggy, which is similar to the LOGO turtle (courtesy Economatics Ltd)

handled in some way (which will be machine-dependent) and all inputs checked rigorously for validity. Cases such as text being entered where numbers were expected must be covered, and the common mistake of pressing Enter before the data (PETS for example, stop a BASIC program if Enter is pressed on its own in response to an INPUT instruction). Under no circumstances should a child see machine generated error messages such as Type Mismatch, Redo?, Extra

Ignored or Division by Zero. If these occur it is the programmer's fault, not the child's.

Children adapt to computers very quickly and at a surprizingly early age. The turtle graphics of LOGO was described earlier in Chapter 4. Children of seven and eight can understand, and use LOGO. An interesting development is a real life 'turtle'; the BBC buggy of Figure 7.3 is driven with LOGO instructions, and can produce patterns with a pen attached to its body.

Children's interest in computers is not without its dangers. Psychologists have remarked on cases where introverted children have become totally involved with computers to the exclusion of all other activities. Adults have also become addicted; most computer organizations have their 'midnight programmers'.

Few people would disagree with the idea of computers in schools, but it would seem that the first flush of enthusiasm may be wearing off. Lady Ada Lovelace's words at the beginning of this book are particularly relevant. It is true, though, that the computer time available to any child at school will be limited, and the purchase of a home computer is an excellent investment for a child's future.

Word processors

To some extent, word processors have been the success story of microcomputing. The economics of selling microcomputer hardware and software suggest that an ideal computer application should meet the following criteria:

1. Many potential customers so development costs can be spread.
2. Each customers requirements to be the same, so there are no modification costs to be included in each sale.
3. Minimal and standard hardware requirements.

The word processor meets each of the above criteria.

In its simplest form a word processor is a glorified typewriter. Text is entered from a keyboard onto a TV screen. The text can be viewed on the screen and errors corrected using editing facilities provided with the word processor, obviating the need for the white correcting fluid used by conventional typists. When the text is correct on the screen it can be printed out, with no errors and no unsightly corrections. The text can also be stored on some form of backing store so that it can be recalled and corrections made at a later date.

A home microcomputer can be used as a very effective word processor, but there are a few hardware requirements to be met if it is to be used seriously. The first is a good monitor; a line of text on A4 paper requires about 70 characters. The standard word-processing display is 80 × 40 characters, which is beyond the resolution of a domestic television.

The next requirement is really at least one disk drive. If it is not possible to quickly load and save text from backup storage, most of the benefits of word processing will be lost. It is possible to store small letters on cassette tapes, but a lengthy report will take a prohibitively long time.

Print quality is important for letters and reports, so a daisy wheel printer is mandatory for serious word processing. High-speed printers are usually not necessary, 300 baud being quite adequate.

A word-processor program for a microcomputer will allow text to be edited, corrected and stored as described above. Additional features such as automatic centring of headings, alignments of left *and* right margins (called justification) are also commonly provided.

In commercial applications, most letters are simply repetitions of standard letters with a few details changed. Word processors allow a standard letter format to be stored. When required, a format can be loaded from disk and the relevant details quickly added to form a new letter.

The format is brought up onto the screen as below, and all the XX positions replaced with the desired text. An XX is included after 'Yours' so 'faithfully' can be used if the letter starts 'Dear Sir' or 'sincerely' if it starts 'Dear Mr. Smith'.

```
    XX                           Deadbeat Engineering,
    XX                           Swale
    XX                           Kent
    Ref;XX                       XX/XX/XX

    Dear XX
                      Accout Ref XX
                      Amount XX
                      Date XX
```

According to our records, the above account in respect of the supply of XX has not yet been received. We would remind you that the terms of purchase were XX days net and we look forward to an early settlement.

Yours XX
XX

An interesting development of the word processor is the inclusion of a spelling dictionary. This checks words against its dictionary and queries any apparent mispellings. This is a boon for typists, as it is very easy to accidentally interchange letters (sepll instead of spell, for example). If the user enters technical or obscure words which are queried, the program can be told to add the new words to the dictionary for future use.

The next obvious stage is the grammar checker. Prototype versions of word processors with dictionaries and grammatical analysis are already available. These will analyse the text for spelling and grammatical errors, and suggest improvements. Style analysis programs are also being developed, which can improve text which is grammatically correct, but awkward.

Small-business systems

Unless a family's finances are unusually complex, a computer is of little use in assisting with home economics. Few people anyway would have the patience to religiously enter the data that the computer would require at regular intervals. Microcomputers can, however, be a great boon to the small business or corner shop. As an added bonus, a word processor will be obtained almost free of charge at the same time.

The first-time user of a small-business machine tends to buy a machine first, then think of uses for it. This is really the wrong way round. The prime reason for buying a machine should be carefully studied and a market survey of available software undertaken. The choice of the actual computer should be the last decision made.

A business computer system should not be done on the cheap. Excellent home computers such as the Oric, Spectrum and the like do not have the keyboard and other

Figure 7.4. A typical small-business machine with computer, twin disks and printer (courtesy Commodore Business Machines)

facilities needed for a business machine. A full-size typewriter-style keyboard and a monitor (as opposed to a domestic TV) are essential, as are a printer and dual disk drives. It is possible to manage with a single disk drive, but disk backups become tedious. If finances permit, standard (as opposed to mini) floppies should be used. Data tends to grow at a surprising rate, so the more space the better. The ideal back-up storage is a solid Winchester disk, but this is probably prohibitively expensive for the corner shop.

Apart from the obvious word processing, there are many useful business programs. Not all will, of course, be useful to everyone but the examples below should serve to show the type of applications that can be computerized.

Most businesses get tied up in a dreary trail of official paperwork with VAT, National Insurance and Income Tax. These are usually the first activities that people consider relinquishing to the machine, and there are many programs on the market. Related to these are the spectres of finance and cashflow. Financial planning programs and the ubiquitous spread sheet allow the financial future of a firm to be modelled, and provide the answer to questions such as 'If sales increase by 15 per cent in August, what effects will this have on cash flow and raw materials stocks?' Delivery times of components and invoice delays make such predictions difficult without a computer.

Time and resources are important where a fairly complex job has to be completed by a certain date. These can be managed by a technique known variously as Critical Path Analysis (CPA) or Programme Evaluation and Review Technique (PERT). This analyses interactions such as 'the roof cannot be erected until the walls are up' and 'there is an 8-week delivery on the door lintels' to predict how long a complex job will take, which items are 'critical' and which have slack time. It is also possible to use CPA to predict, and optimize, labour requirements (e.g. if we move the hydraulic piping back by two weeks it will not affect the delivery time as it has three weeks' float, and we can use the engineers who will have finished the water pipework by then). It is possible to do this analysis by hand with charts similar to Figure 7.5, but computer methods are quicker and allow progress to be reviewed daily if required, and 'What if?' investigations to be made.

A database is an organized collection of data, similar in principle to a card index system. Many businesses require some form of ordered storage of data that can be quickly accessed; a freelance photographer and his negatives, blueprints in an engineering workshop, data sheets in an electronic component shop. General-purpose database programs allow the user to build up a file on a disk and access it from any desired key. A user with a file of technical article titles and precis might ask 'what articles are there on the effect of

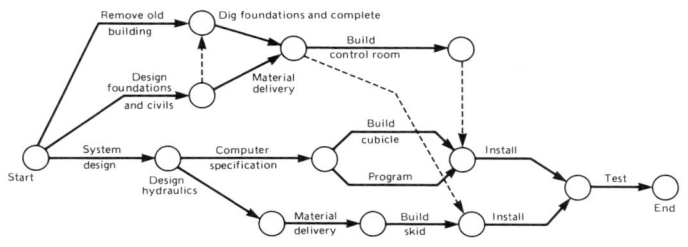

Figure 7.5. A PERT chart (most are far more complex than this)

electric arc furnaces on light flicker?' and the database would display relevant article titles. The difficult part of getting a database working usefully is loading all the data. This should be viewed as a long-term operation.

Keeping track of stock and supplies is often a problem, and a stock-control program can help a user with many items to be controlled. Using simple minimum bin levels and a knowledge of delivery times it can keep stock at an economic level. Stock movement can also be analysed to show which items are being used, and which are sitting on the shelf costing money in storage and bank interest.

Mailing lists are of interest not only to firms but also to clubs and other organizations. At its simplest, a mailing list will produce address labels for envelopes. More sophisticated programs can produce personalized letters to people who are selected in some way. A trivial example could be a Christmas thankyou letter: 'Dear XX, Thank you for the XX you sent me for Christmas. It was just what I wanted'. The advertising implications are obvious.

There are many other programs: graphical packages for producing printed graphs, bar and pie charts; computer-aided design packages for engineers, scientists and even plumbers; specialist programs for farmers, accountants, newsagents, hotels, dentists and so on. The range is endless.

There are a few important DOs and DON'Ts when considering buying a computer for a small business.

1. Think what you are trying to achieve. Study what's available and do not buy a machine first then look for programs after.
2. Do not try to write your programs yourself at first unless your prime reason for buying the machine is to learn about computing.
3. Do not use a neighbour's son who has just done A-level Computer Studies. Friendships can get very strained when the inevitable bugs appear.
4. Try to see how other users manage with the software you're considering; do not buy blind.
5. Make disk backups with regularity.
6. Ensure that the computer is your servant, not your master.

For a tax-deductable outlay of one or two thousand pounds, a small firm can have a word processor, filing secretary, technical assistant, wages clerk and librarian. The business microcomputer will be one of the growth areas of the next decade.

Information technology

Integrated circuits and digital electronics are the technologies that are responsible for the growth of the microcomputer. They are also responsible for the even more impressive growth of the topic known as Information Technology, a grand name covering the marriage of television, telephones and the computer to bring a whole host of services to the home and business.

The simplest of these is Teletext, the news/information service transmitted under the name Ceefax by BBC and Oracle by ITV. The service transmits digital signals on unused lines on a TV picture (the Teletext signal can be seen as a pattern of flashing dots at the top of the picture by adjusting the television height control). These digital signals are used to produce pages of text at the receiver. Each page consists of 24 rows of 40 characters per row; eight colours and a useful selection of block graphic symbols are available.

To access Teletext, the user selects Teletext mode and dials up the required page number (e.g. page 102 is currently news headlines on Ceefax). Pages are transmitted in sequence, and when the selected page number is received the Teletext circuit accepts the data, stores it and displays the page on the screen.

It takes approximately 0.25 second to transmit a page, so with a typical 'magazine' of between 100 and 200 pages there may be a delay of about 30 seconds before a page comes round. In practice, common pages such as the Index or news headlines are transmitted every few seconds.

Televisions are available with built-in printers which can print out selected pages at predetermined times. It is possible that the newspaper of the future may be transmitted rather than delivered.

An interesting development of Teletext is Telesoftware, currently on commercial trial by the BBC. Computer programs, in a dialect of BASIC, are transmitted as standard Teletext pages and can be received and stored by a computer with a suitable Teletext decoder. At the time of writing the decoders are quite expensive, and the programs being transmitted are of a very educational nature, so the service would appear to be aimed at schools rather than the home user.

Interesting experiments are also taking place on the feasibility of transmitting computer programs as audio tones over domestic VHF radio channels. The programs are transmitted as tones in the same way as they are recorded on a cassette recorder. To overcome dialect problems between different versions of BASIC, a 'translator' program is available to convert the transmitted BASIC program to the version of BASIC used on the receiving machine.

Telesoftware, Teletext and VHF program transmission all have limitations. Telesoftware and Teletext are limited by the number of pages available, which is determined by the access time taken for any given page to come round. Obviously the more pages the longer the potential wait. VHF programs are only available at specific times, usually late at night to avoid annoying other listeners. All suffer from interference to various degrees.

The public telephone network gets round these problems and gives almost instantaneous access to a vast collection of programs and information. In the UK, this service is called PRESTEL, which is accessed via the public telephone network and a modem (see Chapter 2). A domestic television is used for the display, and a small dedicated keyboard for input.

PRESTEL is rather business-orientated, being largely concerned with share prices, travel arrangements and specialized information. PRESTEL does, however, have a related computer user's service called MICRONET. This connects a home computer to the PRESTEL computer, and gives access to programs, information, direct ordering of goods, electronic mail and so on. At the time of writing, MICRONET costs about £1 per week plus, of course, the telephone calls to PRESTEL. For most people this is a local call. Access to PRESTEL services is also available via MICRONET, but PRESTEL services have to be paid for on a page-by-page basis.

Interconnection of computers to form networks will be one of the obvious growth areas of the next decade. Systems such as the BBC ECONET allow educational establishments to link students' and teachers' machines to form a school computer network. It is also possible to view catalogues and order goods directly via computer networks (the price being directly debited from your bank account or credit card). One enterprising building society is already offering a free PRESTEL terminal and subscription with accounts over a certain amount.

Dedicated microcomputers

The microprocessor is often through of as a 'computer on a chip'. This is erroneous, as will have been gathered, because a microprocessor needs a store, input/output circuits and many pieces of other equipment to produce a useful machine called a microcomputer.

There are, however, devices which are true computers on a single integrated circuit, and these occur in surprising places. These microcomputers contain all the components of a very small (1 K store) computer except the power supply in one integrated circuit *including* the program stored permanently in a ROM, also in the IC.

These are not of interest to the home user, because the manufacturers will only produce them in very large quantities. The manufacturing processes to produce ICs involve a lot of design and tooling costs. The first IC of a new type may cost several hundred thousand pounds, the second a few pence. Production runs must therefore be large to make the whole operation cost-effective.

Large production runs are, however, normal for motor car firms, domestic appliance manufacturers and similar organizations. Dedicated single-chip computers are appearing in washing machines (replacing the troublesome electromechanical programmer), cookers, motor car trip computers and MPG indicators, burglar alarms and intelligent central-heating controllers to name just a few applications. They are even appearing in toys; the Big Trak of Figure 7.6 uses a single chip computer (and rather interestingly its movements can be programmed by a child in a simple form of LOGO, described earlier in Chapter 4).

The future

It is certain that the computer is going to have more and more impact on our lives. It is also certain that computers will become more powerful. In general, the power of a computer is determined by three factors: speed, the ease of programming and the amount of data that can be stored.

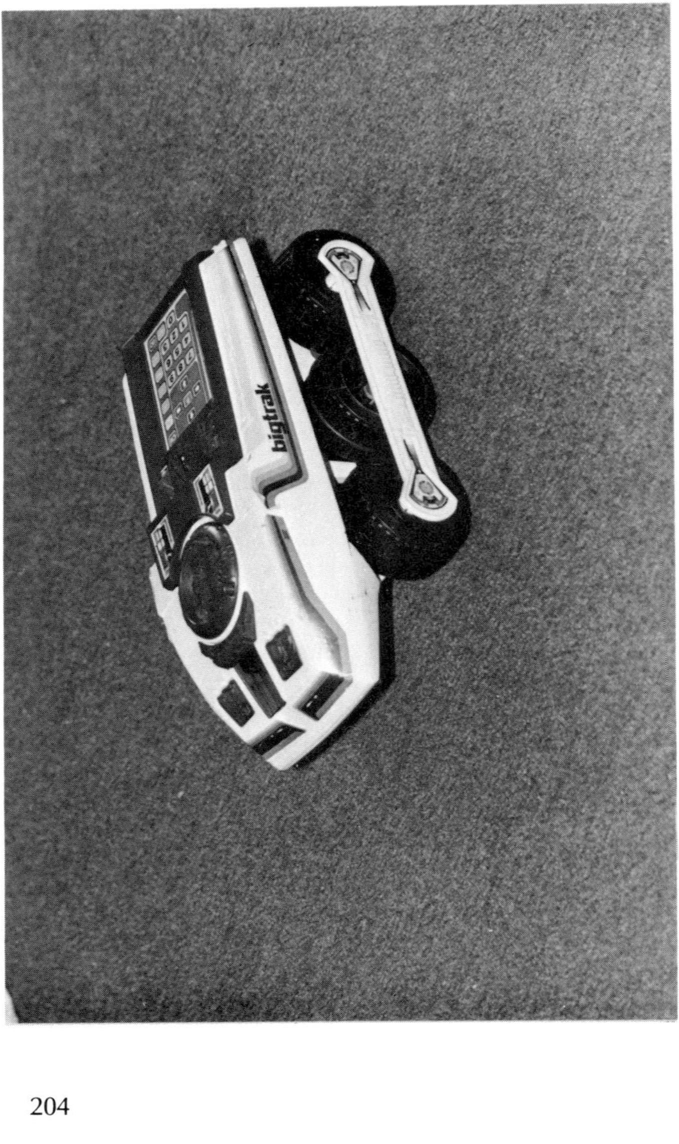

Figure 7.6. An application of a dedicated microcomputer; the bigtrak uses a TMS 1000 computer on a chip

Speed is determined by the physical dimension of the computer. Integrated circuits operate so fast that they have to wait for electrical signals to pass down wires. The smaller the circuit, the faster it can operate. It is currently thought that today's technology will allow an increase of ten in the 'packing density' on an integrated circuit. At this density, several Bibles could be written on a pinhead. Faster and cheaper computers will result, and computers will appear in more applications.

Programming a computer has always been thought a complicated matter. Early computers were difficult beasts, but the popularity of home computers shows that anyone can control a computer. In the future, computers will become easier, and friendlier to program, and languages will come closer to flowing English.

The key to storage is not so much the RAM, but the backing store. Bubble memories and Winchester disks are already available, giving respectively storage without power and cheap Megabyte (one million character) storage. Research suggests that storage at the atomic level may be possible. Cheap bulk storage will probably have as much impact on the future of computing as the microprocessor itself.

This all sounds rather foreboding and Orwellian. It is true there is a danger in vast Governmental data banks. One of the greatest weapons the public has is knowledge, and knowledge of computers gained from a Spectrum or a VIC may, indirectly, prevent the instigation of a computer-run police state.

Index

Address (store), 14
Algorithms, 109
Amphenol plug, 37
Analog signals, 54
Analytical engine, 1
Arrays, 92, 97
ASCII, 35, 36
Assembler, 143

Babbage, 1
Backups, 160
BASIC
  arrays, 92, 97
  functions, 98
  introduction, 58
  line numbers, 65
  modifying programs, 67
  printing messages, 64
BASIC functions
  ABS, 99
  general, 98
  INT, 98
  LEFT$, 90
  LEN, 88
  mathematical, 99
  MID$, 90
  RIGHT$, 90
  STR$, 90
  SQR, 98
  trigonometrical, 99

BASIC keywords
  DIM, 94
  FOR/NEXT, 77
  GOSUB, 81
  GOTO, 73
  IF/THEN, 74
  INPUT, 71
  LET, 60, 69
  LIST, 66
  NEW, 66
  PRINT, 33, 60, 64, 70
  READ/DATA, 95
  REM, 73
  RESTORE, 96
  RETURN, 82
  STEP, 78
  STOP, 83
Baud rate, 40
BBC Buggy, 193
Binary, 18
Bit, 19
Brackets ( ), 33
Bubble sort, 109
Business applications, 196
Byte, 19

Cassette
  digital, 51
  files, 148
  recorders, 26

Centronics interface, 37
Close (files), 160
COBOL, 140
Colour graphics, 179
COMAL, 121, 137
Combiner, video, 30
Compilers, 121
Computer
  applications, 189
  as a calculator, 33
  choosing, 21
  dedicated, 203
  early, 2
  education, 190
  languages, 58
  micro, 4, 11
  mini, 3
  parts of, 6, 13
Connectors, tape recorder, 27
Connectors, printers, 37
Copy (files), 160
CPA, 198
Critical path analysis, 198

D-type connector, 37
Daisy wheel, 41
Database, 147
Debugging, 114
DIN plugs, 28, 37
Direct mode, 34
Disk drives
  applications, 144
  field, 147
  file, 147
  floppy, 47
  general, 45, 144
  hard sector, 48
  items, 147
  operating system (DOS), 152
  records, 146
  sectors, 47
  soft sector, 48
  tracks, 47
Domino connector, 37
DOS, 152
Dot matrix printer, 42

DRAW, 176
Drum graph plotter, 45

Editor, 122
Envelope, 186

Field, 147, 156
File, 147
File names, 153
FILL, 177
Financial planning, 198
Fixed-length record, 9, 156
Floppy disk, 47
Flow chart, 9, 10, 106
FORMAT, 160
FORTH, 130
FORTRAN, 123
Full duplex, 56

Games
  adventure, 184
  arcade, 183
  chess, 182
  general, 161
  player inputs, 180
  speed, 112
GET$, 181
Graph plotter, 45
Graphics
  block, 166, 167
  colour, 179
  general, 166
  high-resolution, 174
  line, 167, 174
  pixel, 167, 172
  sprites, 170
  turtle, 125
  user-defined characters, 168
Graphics tablets, 54

Half duplex, 56
Handshake, 36
Hard sector, 48
Hex, 20
High-resolution graphics, 174

Immediate mode, 34
Indexed file, 148
Information technology, 200
INK, 180
INKEY$, 181
Integer variables, 85
Integrated circuits, 4
Interpreters, 121
Items, 147

Joysticks, 181

K, 17
Keywords, 68

Languages
  ADA, 141
  assembler, 143
  BASIC, 58
  BCPL, 141
  C, 140
  COBOL, 140
  COMAL, 121, 137
  FORTH, 130
  FORTRAN, 123
  general, 123
  LISP, 139
  LOGO, 125
  machine code, 141
  PASCAL, 121, 134
  PILOT, 141
  PROLOG, 140
  turtle graphics, 125
Light pen, 51
Line graphics, 167, 174
Line numbers, 65
LISP, 139
LOGO, 125
Loops, 77
Loops, nested, 80

Menu-driven programs, 52, 110
Memory, 14

MEP, 5
Microcomputer, 4
Microdrive, 51
Micronet, 202
Microprocessor, 4
Minicomputer, 3
Minidisk, 47
Modems, 55, 202
Modulation, 31
Monitor TV, 25, 32
MOVE, 176

Nested loops, 80
Nested subroutines, 84
Networks, 202

Object program, 122
Octal, 18
Open (files), 154
Operating system, 17
Operating system (DISK), 152

PAPER, 180
Parallel, 36
Parity, 40
PASCAL, 121, 134
Passwords, 153
Peripherals, 34
PERT, 198
Phono plug, 28
Pitch, 185
Pixel graphics, 167, 172
Player inputs, 180
Prestel, 202
Printers
  baud rate, 40
  connections, 37
  daisy wheel, 41
  general, 35
  matrix, 42
  parallel, 36
  serial, 36
Procedures, 120

Programming
  algorithms, 109
  BASIC, 58
  debugging, 114
  flow chart, 106
  for speed, 112
  introduction, 16
  menu-driven programs, 52, 110
  procedures, 120
  structured, 119
  style, 118
  top down, 104
  writing programs, 102
Prompt, 29

Random-access file, 148, 156
Random-access memory, 16
Random number, 99
RAM, 16
Read only memory, 16
Real variables, 84
Records, 146
ROM, 16
RPG, 141
RS 232, 37

Sector, 47
Serial, 36
Serial-access file, 148, 154
Serially accessed memory, 16
Simplex, 56
Soft sector, 48
Sorting, 109
Sound, 185
Source program, 122
Spaghetti programming, 73
Speed (of programs), 112
Spread sheets, 198
Sprites, 170
Stack, 130
Stock control, 199

Store
  description, 14
  machine code, 141
  RAM, 16
  ROM, 16
  size, 17
String variables, 86
Strings, 59
Stringy floppy, 51
Structured programming, 119
Subroutines, 81
Systems analysis, 103

Tablet, graphics, 54
Tape recorders, 26
  connections, 27
  digital, 51
Telephone networks, 55
Teletext, 201
Top-down programming, 104
Touch screen, 53
Track, 47
Turtle graphics, 125
TV display, 25, 29, 162

User-defined characters, 168
Utilities (disk), 160

V 24, 37
Variables, 59, 62
Variables, naming, 59, 63
  real and integer, 84
  string, 86
Vector graphics, 178
VERIFY, 29
Video combiner, 30
Video RAM, 163, 171

Word, 19
Word processors, 194

20mA printer, 37